FISHERMAN'S
PARADISE

FISHERMAN'S PARADISE

Tales of Taupo Rainbows

O. S. HINTZ

with an Introduction by
VISCOUNT COBHAM
K.G. G.C.M.G.

MAX REINHARDT
LONDON SYDNEY
TORONTO

© O. S. Hintz 1975
ISBN 0 370 10486 2
Printed and bound in Great Britain for
Max Reinhardt Ltd
9 Bow Street, London WC2E 7AL
by W & J Mackay Ltd, Chatham
Set in Monotype Bembo
First published 1975

CONTENTS

*Eight pages of photographs
follow page 96*

'...AND NO FISH'

Fisherman's Luck is normally defined
Monosyllabically, in language crude.
A pity that a pastime so refined
Should suffer phraseology so rude.
    Some folk may think it borders on the lewd.

The clammy trousers clinging to the seat;
The nagging fear of fibrositic pain;
The empty-handed, mortified retreat
From pools where every fly was cast in vain.
    Did someone say that fishermen are sane?

So when my friends from distant parts send greeting,
Wishing me fortune's joy with rod and reel,
The Angler's Epilogue can stand repeating
In terms to make frustration more genteel:
    'A Wet Posterior and an Empty Creel!'

AUTHOR'S NOTE

My first fishing book, *Trout at Taupo*, was published initially in 1955 and has since run through several printings, with a new and enlarged edition in 1964. Over the span of nearly twenty years various friends and fellow fishermen have urged me to produce, if not a sequel, at least another Taupo book.

Retirement from a fairly exacting profession, along with permanent residence at Taupo, have at last provided the spur. My friends have been right in insisting that Taupo is such a tremendous fishery and the tales associated with it so many that it is well nigh impossible to do it justice within the confines of a single book.

Moreover, all of us who fish at Taupo have witnessed during the past twenty years many developments that merit some detailed study and critical appraisal.

I make no apology for having introduced into the following pages certain aspects of angling politics. For centuries, perhaps, mankind has been prone to regard the lakes and rivers of inhabited lands with that familiarity which is said to breed contempt, but only in relatively recent times has contempt exploded into ugly and wanton desecration. Politicians and bureaucrats, awakened to the danger, have been forced to take action, often reluctant action; anglers and other conservationists have consequently been forced to enter the dusty arena of politics to ensure that action is adequate and effective for the ends that must be achieved.

Still less need I apologise for my attempts to portray the Maori people of Taupo as members of a race fully deserving of understanding, respect and affection. Among them I have been fortunate enough to make many good friends. Without its Maori background Taupo would certainly lose some of its charm. For those interested in a more detailed study of Taupo Maoridom, I commend Sir John Grace's admirable book, *Tuwharetoa*, an authoritative history of the tribe in which Grace himself holds high hereditary rank. I owe much to Grace's work as a source of confirmation and elaboration for many of the tales that have been told to me by my Maori friends.

I am indebted to Mr P. J. Burstall, Conservator of Wildlife for the Rotorua-Taupo conservancy, for his help in checking the initial typescript of this book for factual errors that I might have perpetrated. Pat Burstall is an acknowledged authority on Rainbow trout and a fisheries manager of rare capacity and discernment. He has advised me on matters of fact, but he is in no sense involved in questions of opinion which represent views that are entirely my own.

The photographic illustrations that accompany the text are reproduced by courtesy and kind permission of the proprietors of the New Zealand Herald (my own old newspaper) and the National Publicity Studios of the New Zealand Government.

A friend of long standing, Mrs Betty Brookes, has specially drawn the black and white sketches of Taupo scenes and Taupo flies that serve as headpieces and tailpieces for the chapters of the book. I owe her a special debt of gratitude.

O.S.H.
Rainbow Point, Taupo
April 1974

INTRODUCTION

by Viscount Cobham, K.G., G.C.M.G.

All those, and their name is legion, who love New Zealand and New Zealand fishing will welcome a successor to *Trout at Taupo*. My old friend 'Budge' Hintz is worthy to be called the Izaak Walton of New Zealand; like the old maestro he realises that to all true anglers the fish is merely the central figure in a pageant of river and countryside, of still places and rushing water, and less frequently of still water and tempestuous wind.

No art is complete without humour, and fishing provides it in full measure for its devotees. There is literally no end to the permutations achievable by an angler, 120 yards of cast, line and backing, and a fighting fish. I myself saw, only last year, a passionate but rather lumbaginous octogenarian standing in a quiet pool and playing a heavy salmon in the pool below him and at a right-angle, whilst sixty yards of line see-sawed across a waste of sand, rock and scrubgrass; unbelievably he landed his fish some twenty minutes later. But where, other than in New Zealand, can a man ever have fished from a horse?

It is true to say, however, that New Zealand can rightfully be called 'Fisherman's Paradise'. Her lakes, rivers and streams teem with big fish, both rainbow and 'brownies', and they can be pursued with both wet and dry flies, although the latter are predominantly for use in the South Island.

I was interested to learn that the author's main loves are the Waitahanui and the Tongariro rivers. Many 'locals' and perhaps most visitors extol the virtues of the Tauranga-Taupo. This is certainly a lovely stream, but for me it lacked the intimacy of the Waitahanui and the challenge of the great Tongariro (as Sir Winston Churchill once wrote of President Hindenburg, 'The name itself is massive').

Nobody writes of New Zealand and fishing with more charm and authority than Mr Hintz. For all who practise the gentle art, for those for whom, like myself, New Zealand has laid her gentle and immortal spell, this book will revive nostalgic memories, and enquiries from our nearest travel agent.

FISHERMAN'S
PARADISE

I

RAINBOW COUNTRY

A wise man once said that 'if you're too busy to go fishing, you're too busy'.

Certain devout Moslems likewise believe that Allah does not count against a man's allotted span the hours and days that he spends fishing.

And old Izaak himself could note with approval the observation of his learned friend, Sir Henry Wotton, 'a most dear lover and frequent practiser of the art of Angling; of which he would say, "'Twas an employment for his idle time which was then not idly spent."'

Closer to our own times comes Viscount Grey of Fallodon. He reached the conclusion that 'any really keen angler who has not had to work from necessity, and yet has not spent the whole of each season in fly fishing, may say, as Clive said when he reflected on his opportunities of acquiring wealth in India, that he is astonished at his own moderation'.

All such distilled wisdom gives aid and comfort to one who, in retirement, has chosen to live permanently in fisherman's country and to fish as and when the spirit moves him. I am no longer too busy to go fishing. If the generosity of Allah extends to distant infidels, my days will be long. My idle time need never be idly spent. And yet, with ample leisure to fish, I am astonished at my own moderation.

Fly fishing has been part of my life for more than half the years already reckoned against me. For forty-five years, war service excluded, I earned my living and found great personal satisfaction in daily journalism. My whole working life was spent with one large morning newspaper. For more than half of those forty-five years I held executive positions, culminating in 11 years of responsibility as editor.

By the very nature of his work, a newspaper man gets very little free time and guards it jealously when he gets it. As far as I could, I used to plan my working years to allow myself three full weeks of annual holiday in our antipodean autumn and to spend the whole of that precious time at Taupo, in Rainbow country, fishing from dawn till dark for the finest sporting fish I have ever encountered and recharging mental and physical batteries for the not inconsiderable labours of the ensuing months.

In an earlier book I have written about some of those fishing holidays in what still remains a fisherman's paradise. The great years of the Taupo fishery admittedly belong to the storied past. That seems to happen with every stretch of virgin water into which trout are introduced and acclimatised. Initially the lakes and rivers carry prodigious feed stocks—larvae and insects, small indigenous fish, crustacea and the like. For the early immigrant trout every day is a feast day. They gorge themselves on the abundant food supply, wax fat and strong and so continue until their

14

own numbers so increase by natural spawning that a depleted food supply proves inadequate to sustain the gargantuan growth of the early years.

Such has been the experience in most New Zealand waters. It has been the experience, too, in the Snowy Mountains area of Australia where man-made lakes at first yielded tremendous fish by local standards, with a steady decline in length and weight as the natural larder became less bounteous. Doubtless the same thing will happen, if it is not already happening, in the mountain lakes and rivers of Argentina and Chile.

Of all this, more anon. The important thing is that a high standard of size and condition can be achieved and maintained in any acclimatised trout stock by an unremitting attention to natural food supplies and by an intelligent application of flexible rules and regulations governing the harvesting of the stock by anglers.

And so back to our Taupo trout. I started fishing for them in 1935. Even in a hard season they still fascinate and delight one who has never stopped and who never will stop learning fresh things about them. One of the things that I have learned is that freedom and leisure to fish for trout the year round produces a new mental approach to the gentle art of angling—a gentler approach and a more philosophical detachment.

In the years that are past, weather and other circumstances permitting, a fishing holiday demanded a constant attendance on the water, with only forced interludes for eating, drinking and sleeping. A consuming passion had to be concentrated within a limited space of time. You could spend a whole year dreaming of trout and preparing for trout—winter weekends checking gear and tackle, hours devoted to the output of the most cunningly fashioned flies, bedside reading of fishing books and tackle dealers' catalogues. Then would come escape from the city, the eager, anticipatory drive through the pleasant countryside and the joyous arrival at the great lake with its sparkling rivers and its vast store of trout. All you needed were the skill, the persistence and the luck to take your share of them.

Taupo has held trout for less than a hundred years. The Brown trout came first, in the 1890s. They were the descendants of fish hatched in Tasmania from the imported ova of trout stripped on famous English rivers. Stock from Tasmania was successfully acclimatised in the South Island of New Zealand in 1868, but some twenty years passed before liberations were made in Taupo. Not long before that time Rainbow trout from North America had been introduced into the North Island and in the closing years of the nineteenth century fry from a hatchery about sixty miles away were liberated in Taupo.

About the origins of the trout, particularly of the Rainbow, a certain amount of confusion has developed. The early enthusiasts of the acclimatisation societies in New Zealand did not bother overmuch with the keeping of detailed and accurate records. It is known that the Auckland Acclimatisation Society, in particular, made numerous attempts to introduce, hatch and rear the ova of various North American species. All early attempts failed until, in 1883, a consignment of healthy ova arrived from San Francisco. The ova were hatched and, after various trials and tribulations, the young fish were successfully reared and liberated.

It is undeniably on record that this successful consignment consisted entirely of steelhead ova. They came exclusively from fish trapped at the hatchery of the Great Western Railway Company near Santa Rosa, on the Russian River, north of San Francisco. The then manager of the hatchery stated subsequently that he personally had collected the ova for shipment and that only steelheads were handled at the hatchery at that time.

As far as I have been able to ascertain—and I have ploughed earnestly through the published authorities on the subject—it was from this one importation in 1883 that all Rainbow stocks in New Zealand waters developed. One authority, the late Derisley F. Hobbs (whom I knew well) stated that 'any small importations of Rainbow ova of different origin, made long after, do not appear to have been released except where fish of the original stock had already become very abundant.'

I have heard it argued that three separate and distinct species of Rainbow exist in Taupo. I refuse to believe it. To me they are all descendants from Russian River stock, and any individual peculiarities in appearance that have developed over the years are simply the result of natural mutations that have occurred in a landlocked habitat.

A few years ago I was taken by American friends on a pilgrimage to the Russian River and viewed a stretch of its sweeping bends and occasional sandbars above and below the swimming pool of the Bohemian Grove. I have never managed to fish the river, because my journeys through the delightful city of San Francisco have never coincided with the steelhead runs which, I gather, generally occur in winter.

On the day of my pilgrimage my host, Ken Morrish, who has fished for Rainbows at Taupo as well as for steel-head on the Russian River, stood with me on a bluff above a great pool, with towering redwoods behind us, and we both paid silent tribute to the men who, eighty-five years earlier, had transplanted fish from those waters to the lakes and rivers of a distant land. I still salute those triumphant pioneers.

The Taupo Rainbow, in my view, is the supreme sporting fish. Admittedly the heaviest and most handsome fish I have ever landed was a Brown. I have done battle with Atlantic salmon and sea trout in Scottish rivers. I have fished for Rainbows, Browns and brook trout in North America. In my own country I have cast flies for trout in many waters other than Taupo. All the evidence convinces me that Lake Tarawera, in the Rotorua district 50 miles to the north of Taupo, today holds our largest Rainbows, but in the main it is a troller's lake (as Taupo, to a lesser extent, is tending to become), and I do not care greatly for boat fishing or, under normal conditions, for still-water angling.

I have never managed to fish for mahseer in India or for the redoubtable tiger fish in Africa. On a Commonwealth Press Conference tour of India and Pakistan in 1961 I tried my damnedest to organise a free day on a river with borrowed gear and the necessary supply of leech repellant. Our Asian hosts were eager to oblige me, but, as so often happens in the East, the expedition after mahseer was always postponed to another day—which failed to arrive. So I cannot compare mahseer and Rainbow. I am simply left with the conviction that no other freshwater fish in my angling experience runs as far or as fast as a well-conditioned Taupo Rainbow taken on the fly, and none fights with a more visible and spectacular display of energy.

Fighting qualities apart, the charm of Taupo fishing lies in the extent and variety of running water in which it is possible to fish for the incomparable Rainbow. The fish are landlocked and use the great lake, which covers 240 square miles at an altitude of nearly 1200 feet, as their sea. The one outlet from Taupo is the long and winding Waikato River, but a few miles north of the point where it flows from the lake the river crashes and thunders over the Huka Falls—a barrier that not even the heaviest and strongest Rainbow could surmount.

But round the lake, every few miles or so, rivers and streams rush down from the encircling hills and plateau to charge the vast natural reservoir and to serve as spawning waters for the trout.

So develops the pattern to which the Taupo fly fisher adjusts himself. For the last several years Taupo has been open for fishing all the year round, with no close season, although the upper reaches of the tributary rivers, beyond normal angling access in most cases, are declared closed waters from the beginning of June until the end of November. The restriction is simply a wise measure of conservation to protect spawners that have successfully run the gauntlet of flies and lures in the lower reaches of the rivers and have thereby fully earned the right to reproduce their kind and to maintain their own legendary stock.

The vast majority of Taupo Rainbows spawn in winter, although fluctuations occur from year to year in accordance with climatic conditions and with variations in the three-year spawning cycle. As a matter purely of convenience, it will probably prove helpful to study the angling pattern of the calendar year.

January is normally a hard month. The rivers in the main are empty, the spawning fish having made their mass downstream migration back to the lake several months earlier. The next generation of spawners is just beginning to congregate round the mouths of the rivers to store themselves with food and to put on condition for their winter spawning run. It is midsummer in the Southern Hemisphere, and the height of the holiday season. Whole families crowd the waters at the river mouths that are restricted to artificial fly only. Even more numerous families, from launches and outboard boats, troll the lake with assorted forms of hardware. Elsewhere, at favoured spots round the lakeshore, others seek feeding fish that may be cruising close inshore in pursuit of shoaling smelt.

The January yield is seldom high, except from boats. I regard it as a month for the holiday makers and generally confine myself nowadays to early morning sorties at a river mouth. In my first full January as a permanent Taupo resident, I made nine expeditions to the Waitahanui Rip—a favoured fishing spot—and did not land a single fish.

Yet it does not pay to be too dogmatic. Some years ago one of my closest fishing friends, on a holiday weekend in late January and from a pool in the Waitahanui River, took the fish of his lifetime, a 17 lb Rainbow in superb condition. As a result, he presented to the local angling club the Dave MacNicol Cup for the heaviest fish of the season. I won it myself a few years later—but not in January.

February in New Zealand is normally the hottest summer month. The Taupo rivers remain virtually barren, but, as the lake temperature rises, the fish tend to congregate more and more round the river mouths, seeking the colder water as well as the more abundant food.

A similar state of affairs continues into March, but by this time of the year the air is beginning to acquire an autumnal tang. The Browns generally start to run and more often than not the vanguard of the spawning Rainbows enters the rivers. The river fishing does not reach its height in March, but as autumn extends through April and May and as winter descends in June the Rainbow runs become progressively heavier.

A new season opens in July, distinguished from the earlier months only by the closing of spawning waters and by the necessity to take out a new annual licence at the modest sum which is all that is demanded of us for our Taupo fishing.

The Rainbow runs can continue through July and August into September, but with the approach of spring the spawning urge virtually ceases, and in October the downstream migration of spent fish generally begins and just as rapidly ends. It seems to be a mass movement of dark, emaciated, hungry fish back to the larder of the lake. An exploration of some of the smaller tributary streams of Taupo in October can reveal that they are literally black with fish. At such times a sudden flood can cause high mortality, not only among the spent fish but also among the fertilised ova and hatched alevins in the upstream redds.

November and December provide chiefly lake fishing, round the river mouths or from the shoreline where both maiden fish and recuperating kelts compete for the boundless food supply afforded by shoaling smelt or, in favoured areas, by the windfall of green beetle. Many of the fish killed in these months of late spring and early summer are in poor condition and still bear the marks of their spawning exertions—the hens with ragged fins and tails and the jacks often with ugly gashes from their spawning battles. But there are maiden fish as well, bright silver and full of fight.

So the standard pattern of the angling year takes shape, but the standard can never be taken for granted as fixed and absolute. Doubtless some folk from year to year fish by the calendar just as others fish daily by the clock. But trout are unpredictable creatures, the Rainbow even more so than the Brown. A normally dull month can inexplicably yield splendid fish, and a month when spawning runs are expected can prove frustratingly barren. The hours of greatest angling pressure are traditionally dawn and sunset—except, perhaps, in the depths of winter. Yet, having fished at dawn and sunset for a week with little success, I have suddenly found the fish charging at the fly in the middle of a blazing March afternoon.

Fishing the year round means more than just studying a calendar and hoping that the standard pattern will repeat itself. It means fishing with hope on every approach to the water and it means fishing with delight in the proud processional of the seasons.

For the angler fated to a succession of fishless days, I was tempted recently to pen a parody of the classic Flanders and Swann commentary on the meteorology of the British Isles:

JANUARY: Put your rod away.
The milling mob's on holiday.

FEBRUARY crowds are less terrific
But all the fish are soporific.

MARCH arrives, but trout are shy;
Seldom seem to take the fly.

APRIL should with fish be blest,
But winds howl in from south and west.

MAY sees children free from school
Splashing round from pool to pool.

JUNE comes in with icy blast.
Rod rings freeze with every cast.

JULY, and trout run up to spawn,
Ignoring flies to dusk from dawn.

AUGUST runs are still unkind.
The fish have just one thought in mind.

SEPTEMBER brings a hint of Spring,
But trout won't look at anything.

OCTOBER, with obnoxious gales,
Stops raining only when it hails.

NOVEMBER: Slabs and kelts abound,
Twenty inches to the pound.

DECEMBER still yields kelts; and then
BLOODY JANUARY AGAIN!

To live at Taupo and to fish at leisure is now my happy
lot. My wife and I took up residence in our brand new
home in January of 1970, and, with my enthusiasm for the
Rainbow as a sporting fish, it seemed singularly appropriate

that the locality in which we have made our home should be known as Rainbow Point.

From the high ground on which the house is built, we look north and west over the northern arm of the lake—Tapuaeharuru Bay. The hills on the western shore are pasture. At night the lights of Taupo town, to the north, become jewelled reflections in the lake. To the east, Tauhara mountain looms like a huge heraldic animal.

A belt of lofty pines shelters our property from the southerly and westerly winds. Even in winter the terrace outside our sitting room is a suntrap from sunrise to sunset. The pumice soil, responsive to my wife's green fingers and to my own untutored digging and mowing, yields flowers and fruit and vegetables. Tuis and bellbirds, the loveliest songsters of the New Zealand bush, visit us in season, as do the friendly fantails, fluttering all over the place in pursuit of invisible insects. Pancho, the venerable family cat, lords it over the whole estate and refuses to give ground to the neighbouring Labradors, collies, Alsatians and other assorted canine breeds who visit us daily. And when I back my car out of the garage in the early morning, or in the forenoon, or at any favourable hour of the day or night, I can be on the Waitahanui River in ten minutes.

We can move further afield if we so desire. The main State highway from Auckland to Wellington skirts the eastern shore of the lake for about 30 miles to the southern townships of Turangi and Tokaanu. Between Taupo town and Turangi eight rivers of varying magnitude and at least a dozen small streams and creeks enter the lake.

River fishermen from Taupo chiefly fish the Waitahanui; from Turangi and Tokaanu they tend to concentrate on the majestic pools of the Tongariro. The smaller rivers, such as the Hinemaiai at Hatepe, the Tauranga-Taupo at Te Rangiita, and the Waimarino and the Waiotaka on toward the Tongariro, are all splendid trout streams in their own right. But from a fixed base or from a permanent residence, it is generally a case of one river or one stream at a time. A journey of anything up to 30 miles from one centre to another merits a full day's fishing at one's destination, with whatever variety of water it affords. One thing is certain: in fishing country the easiest place from which not to catch fish is the driver's seat of a moving car.

The rivers that enter the lake on its western shoreline are less easily accessible. Roads or car tracks lead to one or two of them, like the Kuratau and the Whanganui, but the others, including the quite fabulous Waihaha, require journeys by boat.

Because of proximity and from personal preference, my Taupo fishing chiefly centres on the Waitahanui. In an earlier book I have written about the river in some detail. With the passing of the years it has not changed much. It maintains its eager flow through successive basins of rough scrub country, flanked by high pumice cliffs, and in its lower valley follows a rather tortuous course, although the natural fall of the land ensures a consistent strength of current.

The pools of the Waitahanui are not large, like those on the Tongariro. In many cases, fishing from one bank, it may be necessary for the angler to ford the river to follow a hooked fish downstream, and in such circumstances local knowledge unquestionably pays. The bottom is of pumice and gravel, which makes for easy wading. Indeed, the Waitahanui has spoiled me for rivers that flow over rocky, boulder beds.

For years I used to enjoy my frequent expeditions to the Tongariro, where I generally made a beeline for the Major Jones Pool, a magnificent expanse of water in which a fish, taking a fly anywhere near the head of the pool, can rip a hundred yards of line and backing off the reel in one first, furious, unobstructed dash and still be held within the limits of the pool itself. But, following a car accident in 1969, I am no longer as firm on my pins as I used to be and the boulder bottom of the Major Jones Pool has become something of a hazard.

'Boulders!' Lord Cobham used to say. 'In the Tongariro they are cannon balls, liberally coated with axle grease.'

With the aid of a wading stick and felt-soled sandals over my wader boots, I still manage to negotiate the Tongariro on occasions, but the Waitahanui, in addition to its proximity to the home of my retirement, also offers the added attraction of easy wading. The river, spring fed, is not greatly subject to floods or discoloration, although in recent years it has provided an object lesson in what can happen when man interferes with the natural environment.

Several years ago an enterprising chap acquired a large block of land on the upper Waitahanui and proceeded to break it in for pastoral farming. The venture involved extensive clearing of scrub and liberal applications of artificial fertiliser. With the loss of protective scrub cover over a considerable watershed area, floods, which had previously been rare, became more frequent. Worse was to follow. The run-off of fertiliser from freshly sown pasture produced the inevitable enrichment of the river water. Musk and watercress, which had previously grown lightly along the river banks, suddenly flourished. The resultant mass of vegetation trapped a proportion of the downstream flow of pumice and silt, and very swiftly forced the current into a deeper and more confined flow.

I learned caution from one early experience of the effects. On a holiday trip I was fishing a particular run which generally yielded me fish. The river swung left out of a fairly large pool into a dog-leg stretch, with the water deepening under the left bank. It had been my custom to wade in from the left bank at the head of the run and to fish down close to the left bank for about 15 yards until deeper water forced a diagonal move over toward the right bank. If I hooked a fish I invariably crossed the river and played it from the right bank, although more often than not a second fording was necessary back to the left bank at the tail of the run, where the river conveniently broadened and shallowed.

On the warning expedition I suppose I noticed sub-consciously an unusually heavy growth of musk and water-cress on the right bank. But I waded in as usual at the head of the run and started to swing my fly from right to left into the deep water. Between casts I took an occasional step downstream. I had just taken one such step when a fish suddenly grabbed my fly and in the same instant I found myself slipping forward into deep water yards upstream from where it normally deepened.

Reactions were swift; they had to be. I dropped my retrieved line in the water and with my right hand clamped the reel line hard to the rod butt. Simultaneously and instinctively I reached out with my left hand for a secure hold on the near bank. It was there in the form of a clump of bracken and lupins, unfortunately concealing a generous growth of blackberry.

The fish, at the end of a firmly held line, jumped violently a few times and soon threw the fly. For once I was glad to see a fish go. I tossed my rod on to the bank, with loose line trailing miserably down the current, and then, with a vast heave on the bankside shrubbery, hauled myself clear of the water and ultimately up onto the grass. I made it miraculously without a drop of water down my waders, whereas a shorter man would have taken a gallon or two over the top. My left hand was dripping blood from black-berry gashes, but it didn't seem to matter.

In point of fact I had been in no real danger of anything more than a thorough wetting. The whole dog-leg stretch is no more than 50 yards long and, even in deep waders, I could have floundered and struggled out of it as long as I kept my head.

I rewound line onto my reel, blessed the lacerating blackberry and then gave the changes in the river the detailed inspection that I should have given them earlier. It was quite clear, when I inspected the terrain critically, that the excessive growth of marginal weed on the right bank had forced the main flow of the current still further to the left, scouring a deep gut in what had previously been wadeable water.

I learned my lesson. Ever since then I have given even the most familiar stretches of the river a close inspection before wading them and certainly before trying to cross them. They say that you have never fished a river properly until you have fallen into it at least once, but that does not mean that one should make a habit of immersion.

Mercifully the changes that upstream farming were beginning to impose on the Waitahanui have now ceased. The enterprising landowner has disposed of his holding to forestry interests who have done even more than was asked of them in the provision of marginal cover along the banks of the main river and its tributary streams. A plantation of trees offers protection to a river, whereas pasture on light soils threatens it with both run-off and chemical enrichment.

Little enough attention was paid to the changing character of the Waitahanui at the time, although anglers complained occasionally about discoloured water and were not ignorant of the cause. To some of us, it became abundantly clear that we should all have to take the most active interest in conservation to protect our Taupo rivers—and probably many other rivers as well—from the side effects of human enterprise.

'Water's a funny thing,' says one of the rural characters in John Moore's last and finest novel. 'Thee's got to go along with it, thee carsn't hold it down against its will, any more than thee can hold rubbub down. It comes and it goes. Maybe for as long as a man's lifetime it'll lie there quiet as weed seeds in winter; lie there so still thee'll forget all about it. Then sudden-like it'll come to life and run wild and rampage.'

I have leisure nowadays to study my river closely at all seasons of the year and to concern myself actively in matters of conservation. It all forms part and parcel of the changed approach that retirement brings, especially when retirement is enjoyed in reasonable proximity to favoured trout water.

When fishing opportunities are limited, the day's bag assumes an overriding importance. One fishes not only for enjoyment of the angling scene, but also with an eagerness to catch fish. Limit bags become a seal of success. Fish lost invite the most painstaking inquests into cause and effect, into the probabilities of human error and into ways and means of avoiding such indignities in the future.

Fish hunger no longer plagues me. I confess that when the weather is right and when my own disposition is so inclined, I still enjoy getting out of bed at about four o'clock in the morning, dressing quietly, stowing rod and waders in my car and backing out of my garage for the short drive to the Waitahanui Rip.

Except at holiday times, the Rip in the early mornings is seldom crowded. As summer slips into autumn it may still be dark when a few cars congregate at the roadside near the Rip, still dark while we struggle into waders and light our way with torches across the pumice beach to the lakeside. We enter the water together, perhaps half a dozen of us, casting out into the broken water where the urgent river current spills over a sandbar and meets the restraining pressure from the lake.

It is fun to hook and play a fish in the dark. The trout may take quietly, or they may smash at the fly, depending often, I think, on the strength of the current and on the direction of the wind. Then they run prodigiously. They have the whole unobstructed expanse of the lake in which to fight for their freedom, with no intricacies of bends and shallows, rocks and snags to restrict them, as in a river.

Now and again a fish will move upstream on you, forcing you to reel madly to avoid slack line. But after you tighten on your fish, you move downstream to your right to get the fish clear of the current, passing your line over the heads of other anglers, and then move cautiously back to dry land for the final stages of the battle, with the fish in shallow water. All this, more often than not, in pitch darkness, with the line from your rod tip disappearing into the void and the precise whereabouts of the fish something of a mystery.

You land your fish, kill it, recover your fly, and bury the fish in wet sand, with driftwood or pumice markers, before you wade back to the line of fishermen at the Rip, casting away as the dawn seeps into the eastern sky. And with the first light the fish generally become visible, porpoising in and out of the water and often jumping clear of their own element as if they were awakening to a day of intense activity. They may take boldly, too, with the changing light, and then their fierce runs and frantic leaps, with the rod arching and the line strumming, make the dawn seem all the more splendid.

Occasionally the unexpected happens. One November morning in the first year of my retirement I had the Rip to myself in the dawn hours. It was daylight at five o'clock and about a quarter of an hour later I had a good view of my first fish as it leapt after taking the fly. Then it tore line off the reel in a magnificent run of 80 yards or more. Twice the fish had me out on backing before I finally managed to shorten line and move back toward the beach.

With that, the early morning flock of seagulls appeared. Taupo is as far from the sea of either coast as any place in

New Zealand, but the birds seem to find the wide waters of the lake congenial and appear to be permanent residents, although where they nest I have never discovered.

The gulls circled overhead. I had a tight line on my strong fish, then only about thirty yards away, and all was going well. Suddenly a swooping gull flew straight into my line. It squawked horribly and made a flopping descent onto the water, with its friends squawking round it just as horribly.

'There,' I thought, 'goes my fish.'

All I could do in the circumstances was to play and land the gull. Its left wing had become hopelessly entangled in the line and it flopped desperately about on the water, captive and angry. I reeled it in and beached it, but when I tried to free my line the bird snapped at me viciously and I could see that the process of disentanglement was likely to prove protracted.

I thought again of my fish, felt the free end of my line, and weight and movement were still there. I paid out line to restrain the captive and squawking gull, still an object of great curiosity to its circling fellows, laid my rod down with the reel in my hat to protect it from pumice sand, and then handlined the frustrated fish ashore. It was a good one of $5\frac{1}{2}$ lb, and it had taken a combined land-sea-air operation to land it.

I killed the fish and returned to the captive gull. Some yards of the running section of a forward taper line were wound round and round its wing. It actively resented all attempts at its liberation, but eventually I unravelled line from feathers, threw the bird into the air, and it flew away, closely pursued by its raucous mates. Then I found my line in the most ghastly tangle imaginable. When I had the mess sorted out and back on the reel, it was very nearly time to drive home for breakfast.

The experience was not quite new to me, because twice

previously I had done battle with seagulls at the Waitahanui Rip. The first occasion was on a dawn fishing sortie when, at first light, I hooked a bird on the back cast. To say 'hooked' is not strictly accurate; actually I had hit the bird in flight and the cast had wound itself round the bird to bind its wings. A fellow fisherman helped me to liberate the angry gull.

The second occasion was during a bright forenoon when I was fishing the Rip on my own. I was just starting to bring my line forward from the back cast when I encountered a solid resistance and the rod tip quivered visibly. I turned round to see a gull making an abject descent on the water and to be greeted with shouts of ribaldry and derision from Doggy White and a couple of his friends who had observed the spectacle from the roadside in front of the old Lodge. This time I had to land the bird. The fly had struck it and had become deeply buried in its breast feathers. The roadside scoffers offered me no assistance, and with a fly disgorger I had to lever the hook out of its hold in the downy plumage while the bird pecked at me savagely. A mass of feathers littered the beach before the liberated bird became airborne.

What I have yet to experience, or even to observe, is the hooking of a shag, an event more likely to take place under water than in the air. Quite frequently these days we see shags fishing close inshore round the Rip, diving even into the current in search of fish. They are hungry creatures, these black predators. It is not uncommon to see a shag surface with a fish of at least 2 lb in its beak. It will then rest on the water and perform the most incredible contortions until it finally turns the fish to swallow it head first.

Some of the Rip fishermen customarily use very large flies, and it would never surprise me if a shag, swimming underwater, were to take one of these monstrous lures in mistake for a small fish, as the trout themselves take them.

But presumably the shag knows better than the trout how to distinguish between the natural and the artificial.

The intrusions of waterfowl need not worry us unduly, although shags take a fairly heavy toll of immature trout and the gulls feed voraciously on spawning smelt and thus compete with the trout for a valuable source of food supply. Nevertheless, the trout survive.

For the average fly fisherman these days, limit bags most certainly prove the exception rather than the rule. Even a recent reduction in the daily bag limit from twenty to ten Rainbow trout has not meant any marked increase in the number of anglers who can boast of limits. The stock of trout, as far as one can judge, remains fairly constant, but the number of anglers fishing for them, as measured by licence sales, has increased tremendously and goes on increasing. When more and more fishermen compete for a relatively stable yield of fish, the result must be fewer fish, as the statisticians would say, 'per rod-hour and per rod-day'.

What matters in such circumstances is the quality of the fish. Here the leisured fisherman comes into his own. One learns to accept fishless days as part of the normal and natural turn of events. One knows—or at least one feels confident —that when a Taupo Rainbow condescends to take the fly it will generally be a fish worth taking.

The philosophic approach can be achieved literally by accident. My particular accident was an encounter with a seven-ton truck, and it is not the sort of approach to philosophic fishing that I would personally recommend. After my discharge from hospital, somewhat the worse for wear, a doctor friend who had been keeping a professional eye on me urged me to have two or three weeks at Taupo before I resumed work.

'You've had a fair battering,' he said, 'but a bit of fishing will do you the world of good. The whole of your right side needs exercise, and casting will give it to you. Don't overdo it. An hour or so at a stretch ought to be enough. Use our cottage at Four Mile Bay, and take your gear with you.'

I fished for a fortnight, seldom for more than two hours a day. I started off with my $9\frac{1}{2}$ ft Leonard, the lightest rod in my Taupo armoury, and gradually worked up to the $10\frac{1}{2}$ ft 'Viscount Grey' and the 12 ft 'A. H. E. Wood', both treasures from the House of Hardy. On my second fishing day at the Waitahanui Rip, toward dusk, I hooked a splendid fish. It took all my dressed line and most of my backing, and it fought furiously for a full quarter of an hour before I beached it. On my spring balance, and on Doggy White's scales at the Lodge, it registered $8\frac{1}{2}$ lb—the heaviest fish I had taken for nine years.

So the convalescent fishing proceeded, mostly at the Rip, with occasional river excursions when westerly winds made the Rip unfishable. Never more than an hour in the water without a rest on the beach or on the bank; never more than two fish a day, and plenty of blank days. But the fish I killed averaged 7 lb, and the mere fishing for them was better than hours of physiotherapy.

Taupo and the Waitahanui had always meant much to me, ever since I first started to fish them thirty-three years before. The fortnight of quiet and physically restricted fishing disclosed a new enchantment. Into the car after breakfast, or in the late afternoon, and an easy drive to the water. Into waders and into action, with a new line swishing and glistening in the sunlight and the whole of my damaged right side responding miraculously to the easy rhythm of the casting. A walk ashore to sit down and change a fly, so that even the prescribed rest period was not wasted. Then back into the water, with the rippling of the current and the broad expanse of lake sparkling in the warm autumn sunshine. The high land far away on the western side of the lake would catch the sun in ever-changing variations of colour. Peace and quiet and absolute contentment reposed in the fresh, clean air. I knew that I could manage the few months remaining to the date that I had previously fixed for my retirement.

The few months passed, and we became permanent residents of Taupo, having discovered meanwhile, in the course of building, the new house that was to be and is now our home. The change from a busy city existence to a life of more or less rural retirement was made all the easier by that spell of convalescent fishing which had shown me how simple it is to enjoy one's hours on the water without extending them into a self-imposed labour and without regarding them as gainful or wasted in relation to the number of fish killed.

In our first six months as permanent residents of Taupo, Cara and I took relatively few fish. I suppose we fished, either together or separately, about one day in three. I know from my diary records that I averaged about two hours on the water for every day that I fished. We certainly did not spend all our time fishing. The yield in numbers was not high; it worked out at about a fish every third day, and my highest daily bag was three. But the fish I killed in those first six months up to the end of the 1969–70 season averaged 5½ lb.

Most anglers are familiar with the Corbett Scale of condition factors, even if such mathematical mysteries may baffle the uninitiated. Condition factor is calculated by a precise formula relating weight in pounds to length in inches (heaven knows what will happen when we go all metric), and with printed tables one can read off the relevant figures without liability to mathematical error. Fish with a condition factor of 60 or greater are rated as 'exceptional'; from 50 to 59, 'excellent'; and from 37 to 49, 'average'. Anything below 37 is not worth keeping.

What pleased me was that my fish killed during our first residential season showed an average condition factor of

54.4, well into the 'excellent' class. Oddly enough, the best fish was by no means the heaviest. It was a 4 lb Rainbow hen, but it was only 18 in in length, with a resultant condition factor of 69.

I recall quite clearly the day of the kill—a winter's day of heavy overcast and passing showers in late June. I had arrived on the river at about eleven o'clock in the forenoon, had fished my favourite Flaxbush Pool without result and had forded the current to wade down near the right bank and then take up station in midstream to fish a deep pool at a left-hand bend—a pool that I have always called the Kingfisher because, for as long as I can remember, successive pairs of kingfishers have nested in the high pumice bank on the outer curve of the bend. One normally casts here to the left, across the current which swings the line back to the right for a slow retrieve through the depths of the pool.

Several abortive casts to the left had almost persuaded me that the pool was barren of fish and that I should try elsewhere. On a sudden impulse I tried a cast to the right, toward shallow and rather still water from which, I thought, the current would still swing the fly over to midstream, with a different cover of the pool.

The line swung to the left and straightened, as I had hoped and calculated that it would. I let the fly swim idly for a few seconds, but I had hardly taken more than three or four gathers of line on the retrieve when the rod was nearly pulled from my hand. Almost at the same instant a bright silver fish exploded from the pool. It cavorted in and out of the current for several minutes before it decided on a swift and desperate run downstream. I forded the river back to the left bank at my own known and negotiable crossing, tightened on the fish and eventually landed it about half way down the upper stretch of a reach known as the Parade. I regarded it then as a smallish fish of beautiful proportions, but it was not until I had weighed and measured it and later checked the vital statistics against the Corbett Scale that I realised its exceptional condition.

The fish taught me a lesson, too. More often than not, most of us fish a known pool or reach in accordance with past observation and experience. A cast to left or right, as the case may be, covers the lie—or so we think. We proceed accordingly until we consider that the lie is empty. We do not stop to think that some variation in current, or in water level, or in light may have created an alternative lie and that a change in presentation may discover an unsuspected fish.

Since that one experience, I always fish the Kingfisher Pool and other comparable water where the flow of the current seems appropriate with casts to both left and right. The one thing that I try to avoid, fishing wet fly in our Taupo fashion, is a direct cast, straight down the current and into the pool. Such a presentation, I am convinced, will send most fish, including the somewhat reckless Rainbow, scuttling for cover.

In leisurely, resident fishing, even fish lost cease to matter unduly. There was a time when, if I hooked a fish and lost it, I subjected myself, as a holiday fisherman, to the most critical processes of self-analysis. What had I done wrong? Had I struck the fish firmly enough? Had I held it too tight? Had I manoeuvred to apply sufficient side strain? Nowadays, except when a fish breaks me, I simply jog my memory and recall my old Maori friend, Harry Tahau, now dead.

Harry was an exceptionally good fisherman, a genial character and a natural philosopher. When Harry hooked a fish, at the Rip or in the river, it was all Taupo to a lump of pumice that he would land it. But one can never be certain with trout. Occasionally one would get away, and Harry would quietly retrieve line, inspect his fly and cast to ensure that everything was intact, and would then quietly intone his benediction: 'Good luck to the fish!'

A few days ago, as I write these lines for the first rough draft of this book, I hooked a fish in fairly awkward water. The fish took unexpectedly, as I had been fishing the pool for about a quarter of an hour without a touch; but I struck it firmly enough and it proceeded to give a superlative jumping display in an upstream run, while I dipped the rod tip in precautionary salute at every jump. Then the fish turned and careered downstream—and round a bend.

As quickly as I could, I forded the river, anxiously trying to keep a tight line on the fish. But I had to cross above the bend, and the run of the fish and the flow of the current had obviously taken my line close to the left bank under the marginal cover of musk and watercress. By that time the fish had taken all my thirty-five yards of dressed line and had me out on backing. It was still jumping at intervals as I rounded the bend, wading close to the left bank and working the line clear of weed. Then I started to reel in frantically, recovering all my backing and a yard or two of dressed line, and noticing for the first time a friend, Nigel Morris, fishing downstream just below where my fish had stopped its run.

Suddenly there was an explosion in the water, and Nigel turned round to see what was happening. The fish jumped again and, in that final frantic leap, threw the fly. I reeled in my line and Nigel came walking up the bank.

'It was a bloody monster,' he said. 'I heard a hell of a splash right behind me and, when I turned round, the fish nearly jumped down my waders. It must have gone all of 8 lb.'

'Over six, I'm pretty sure,' I said, as I inspected the fly, still sharp of point and barb. 'But—good luck to the fish.'

Old Harry Tahau's words deserve a place in the vocabulary of all who fish for the joy of fishing. We go through our elaborate and time-honoured ritual, often with the most costly gear and with the most cunningly tied flies, in our efforts to hook trout and, if possible, to land them. But the fish is in its own element, while we are operating in an element not altogether natural to us. Also, if we are anglers in the true sense, we are fishing with gear and tackle light enough to give a hooked fish at least a sporting chance. There can be precious little enjoyment or sense of achievement in winching a fish ashore on a cast strong enough to moor a dinghy.

So, if the hooked fish beats the angler in fair combat and regains its freedom, there need be no self-directed recriminations. The hooking and the playing of a strong Rainbow in swift water provide the real thrill of angling, the peak of physical sensation and mental challenge. The landing and the kill provide, admittedly, the ultimate seal of triumph. But the fish that gets away merits the composure implicit in the observation of old Izaak's Piscator to his scholar: 'Nay, the Trout is not lost; for pray take notice, no man can lose what he never had.'

A fish that breaks me I regard as a different matter. In some way or another, I must have been at fault—a weak hook, a badly tied knot, a frayed cast that should have been checked, observed and discarded, or a wind knot in the cast as a result of sloppy and inexpert casting. In such cases, self-censure serves a useful purpose if it begets a meticulous attention to detail. The fish for which we are angling deserves that measure of respect.

For the reasons stated and for others that will become apparent as my tale proceeds, fishing in the leisure of retirement brings with it a whole host of new and unexpected pleasures. Fish hunger can be exorcised. Fishless days no longer weigh heavily on the mind. One has the leisure to fish where and when one wishes, with a blessed escape from the gushing verbosities of radio and television and telephone to the serenity of a broad lake or a laughing river, with the birds in the trees and the blossom in season on manuka and

38

broom and lupin, and with a sense of absolute contentment when a well-cast line places the fly on the water precisely where it was meant to go.

'For Angling may be said to be so like the Mathematicks that it can never be fully learnt.'

II

GOLDEN PAST

The old Lodge at Waitahanui has gone. For most of my working years it used to serve as my holiday home from home. Not that it was so very old. Fred Fletcher built it courageously in the bleak depression years, back before the Second World War. It stood on leasehold Maori land, backing onto the pleasant little Mangamutu Stream which joins the main Waitahanui River just above the main highway bridge. It was hardly more than a stone's throw from the general location of the Waitahanui Rip.

Where the original Lodge once stood, a petrol filling station now serves the needs of the travelling public, although the old cottages and cabins remain for anglers' accommodation. With an alteration in land titles, the Lodge building itself reverted to the Maori landowners and was shifted bodily along the main highway to a site about half a mile further south where it has become a Maori family residence. It seemed reluctant to move. It blocked the main highway bridge for a time while it was being shifted on trailers, and it paused forlornly for an hour or so outside the Maori school while traffic bypassed it cautiously and while the Maori children cheered the efforts of the removal experts.

Many of us will continue to miss the Lodge and its associations with what now ranks as a Golden Past. For in Fred Fletcher's day angling pressure at Taupo was a good deal lighter than it is today, and the regular guests at the Lodge had brave tales to tell of limit bags, of remarkable fish and of improbable angling adventures. The first fish I ever took from the Waitahanui was hooked and landed practically right outside the Lodge front door. In those days the river swung northward, as it still does, below the main highway bridge, but after flowing for a couple of hundred yards parallel with the lakeshore, as it still flows, in what is known as the Lupin Stretch, it suddenly contracted into a succeeding stretch known as the Narrows, or, in Fred Fletcher's words, 'the Mugs' Pool'.

You hardly had to cast to fish the Narrows; you could almost flick a fly across stream from the track on the right bank. Substantial weed beds fronded lazily under water from either bank. As the fly swung round from a short cast across to the left bank—and if the fish were in the river—the head of an inquisitive trout might appear from beneath the weed, there could be a sudden tightening of the line, and a lively scrap would follow as the fish splashed round in the confined current.

Before the Government took over the Taupo fishing rights from the Tuwharetoa tribe in 1926, the Maoris used to issue their own fishing licences for the Waitahanui River and a licence to fish laid down in print some simple but exemplary rules. From the bridge downstream to the river mouth, no wading was permitted. The Lupin Stretch was generally fished from the left bank, the Narrows from the right; and the rule, meticulously observed, was that the fisherman should take five paces downstream after every cast.

In the days of my Taupo novitiate the old timers still adhered to the Maori rules and the system worked admirably. Half a dozen or so anglers could be fishing the Lupin Stretch at intervals of never less than 25 yards. All of them would be in slow but steady movement downstream —a long, diagonal cast to the right, a slow retrieve and then five paces down the bank before the next cast. At the end of the Lupin Stretch, one could walk back up the track on the left bank to the bridge and start the whole cheerful and orderly process over again. Fewer rods could fish the Narrows, but the same sort of circuit applied. And on both stretches, under favourable conditions, most fishermen generally took fish, with equal opportunities for all.

Conditions have changed, somewhat for the worse. Where the Lupin Stretch once merged into the Narrows, a rock groyne was built some years ago at an angle from the roadside, ostensibly to create a permanent river mouth about 200 or 300 yards short of the spot where the river formerly entered the lake. In point of fact, the river has since tended to extend the spit on the left bank, so that the actual river mouth, depending on lake level, continues to move northward. The Narrows stretch, admittedly, has disappeared and, although the Lupin Stretch remains, it shows considerable variations with changes in river flow, and has also suffered a marked deterioration in angling manners.

For some years, the old Maori rule of no wading in the river northward from the bridge has been tossed into the water. Six or seven anglers will wade waist deep just below the bridge. At intervals downstream, other fishermen will stand, five or six in line abreast across the current, and at the deep pool formed by the groyne jutting out from the roadside acrimony frequently enters into the jostling for position on the part of six or seven eager claimants. From the bridge to the groyne, a distance of about 200 yards, the water can often hold as many as thirty so-called anglers, all of them reefing off line down the current, seldom bothering to cast and industriously trolling at the halt. They maintain station for hours at a time. They dislike making way even when one of their number from an upstream platoon has hooked and is playing a fish.

Nearly forty years have passed since I took my first fish from the Lupin Stretch; and quite a few years have passed since I last fished the water at all seriously. I have not cared to join the present generation of river hogs who would never have been tolerated on the water by the founding fathers of the river. But very soon there may be a change for the better. After mature deliberation, the authorities are proposing to introduce a local regulation which will revive the old Maori rule by banning all wading in a stretch of water which can be fished quite effectively from the bank.

Inevitably, in certain quarters, there will be wailing and even some gnashing of teeth. But in the Anglers' Valhalla, if such a place exists, the old masters of the Waitahanui will sit back happily and nod their approval. In the river itself, fish, no longer line-shy, may consent to rest more than momentarily in some of the holding pools.

Certainly, the regulars among the guests in the early days of the old Lodge would applaud the action of management. They constituted a happy band of fishermen. Even a novice among them, such as I was in those days, would be welcomed into the fraternity as soon as he could establish that he was keen not only to catch fish but also to catch them cleanly.

We lived in small but comfortable rooms at the Lodge. We ate stupendous meals three times a day, with an occasional snack in between if ever the occasion demanded it. A drink before dinner was as much a ceremony as a nightcap before bed; and there were those honest regulars who used to insist on frosty mornings that, after fishing at dawn, a rum and milk was obligatory before breakfast.

Fred Fletcher presided over these genial gatherings for the first dozen or so years that the Lodge was in existence, and a succession of subsequent proprietors maintained the tradition. Fred was a Northcountryman born, but a genuine New Zealander by something more than adoption. Well under age, he had fought in France with the New Zealand Division during the First World War, and lungs weakened by gas finally persuaded him to transfer his outdoor love for the Taupo country into permanent residence.

In some ways we were an odd assortment. Most of us were holiday anglers from the cities, but there would always be a sprinkling of farmers from various parts of the country and also a small contingent of regular visitors from overseas. Two Englishmen from Burma became welcome members of the fraternity. They were in residence one season before the war when I arrived for my annual Taupo vacation. We were yarning after dinner that evening and one of the lads from Burma, an ardent river fisherman, was complaining about the absence of fish.

Fred Fletcher joined us, listened for a while to the lament, and then said that there were tons of fish in the river; all you had to do was to hook them.

'Utter bloody rot,' said Evans. 'I fished today every pool from the Cliff to the Narrows, and I didn't get a single touch. The fish just aren't there.'

'Plenty of fish,' Fred repeated, 'but you've got to hook them.'

'I'll tell you what,' said Evans. 'An even bottle of whisky you can't go out and come back with a fish inside a quarter of an hour.'

'That's a bet,' said Fred. He grabbed his huge Hardy 'Murdoch' from the wall rack. He didn't even bother to get into waders, but charged out of the front door and over the road, roaring to me as he went that I should act as timekeeper.

Exactly twelve minutes later by my watch the front door reopened and Fred reappeared with a dripping and still twitching fish. 'Second cast in the Boat Pool,' he said. 'I'd have been back sooner, but the ruddy fish got tangled up in some weed.'

Evans immediately honoured his bet, and five of us cheerfully emptied the bottle.

Tot's bottle celebrated a different sort of fish and in rather different circumstances. Tot was a retired Indian Army officer, Major Willoughby-Tottenham. Unable to face the English climate after years in India, Tot and his wife had chosen to retire in Fiji, and almost annually they would come to Taupo for a month or so of fishing in the late summer. Tot was an ardent and industrious river fisherman who would proceed from pool to pool almost at the gallop. Mrs Tot took her fishing a good deal more placidly. She would venture forth from the Lodge, carrying rod, sewing basket, book, box of chocolates and cigarettes, and seek a quiet pool on the river. She would spend as much time on the bank as in the water.

All this was during the years just before the war, and at that time much interest centred on the presence in Poi Pool of a large resident fish that for a couple of seasons had defied all efforts to secure its legitimate removal. The fish was easily identified by a large white scar just behind its head. Generally it would lurk in deep water near a high bank, but occasionally it would make excursions round the pool, clearly in search of food.

It was a fish of considerable length but indeterminate condition, and we were all convinced that it was a cannibal and should be removed. But the visible presence of the fish was a challenge to remove it by fair means before we descended to foul, and those of us who used to fish Poi Pool regularly offered it a rich and rare assortment of flies. It ignored them all. Major and Mrs Tot were as keen as any of us to deal with the fish which by that time we all knew as 'the Lodger'.

Three of us were coming back from fishing the Rip one day just before lunch when we saw a female figure hurrying down the road in a cloud of pumice dust and leaving behind her a trail of assorted impedimenta. As she drew nearer we recognised Mrs Tot, dishevelled, gasping but triumphant, and clasping to her bosom—the Lodger.

It was the ugliest fish that any of us had ever seen. Long, certainly—it must have been all of 30 inches—but from its huge and repulsive head the body, with the white scar mark apparently revealing some earlier encounter with a fish spear, tapered down to eel-like proportions. The body colouring was dark and the lateral rainbow markings barely discernible. But the Lodger it most assuredly was, and Mrs Tot babbled incoherently about how it had taken a Parsons' Glory, lunged round the pool and then given itself up.

We all marched round to the back of the Lodge where the Major and Fred, hearing the excited chatter, soon joined us. Fred produced a spring balance and suspended the Lodger by the gills. 'Dead on 9 lb,' he announced.

'And if you cut off the head,' commented Gordon Williams, 'it would go about two and a half.'

'Good God!' said the Major. 'Marvellous! Absolutely bloody marvellous!' And he vanished in a flash to reappear just as rapidly, bearing a virgin bottle of whisky and imploring Fred to fetch some glasses.

Drinks were poured, and we all toasted Mrs Tot and the Lodger with due ceremony. And then Fred noted with dismay that the Major was recorking the bottle.

'I dunno, Major,' he said. 'That fish looks more than 9 lb to me. It's a long time since I used this spring balance, and it could be a bit rusty. Wait till I give it a drop of oil.'

Fred produced an oil can, lubricated the spring and once more impaled the Lodger. He held the ghastly fish aloft, steadying it on the hook with thumb and forefinger and at the same time applying an unobserved downward pull.

'Have a look now, Major,' Fred invited. 'What's the reading?'

'God bless my soul,' said the Major, peering at the scale figures. 'It's a shade over 10 lb.'

He uncorked the bottle and passed it round again.

Even then Fred was not satisfied. A third and final weighing, with the same cunning pressure on the balance, raised the weight to just on 11 lb. And we finished the bottle.

Johnny Sheehan's prize completed a bottle trilogy, although it would certainly not exhaust the number and variety of bottle stories that the old Lodge could tell. Johnny Sheehan was one of the characters of pre-war Taupo, a publican of Irish descent who ran at different times two of the three licensed Taupo hotels. He was a friend of all Taupo fishermen, and one year he announced that he would donate a bottle of whisky for every fish caught during the first month of the season with a weight running into double figures.

The season in those years opened in November, and early one morning during the first week Fred, fishing at the Rip, landed a splendid Rainbow. He bore it back to the Lodge in triumph, convinced that it would win him a bottle of whisky. But an impeccably accurate set of scales would not put it higher than $9\frac{1}{2}$ lb.

'Damn it,' said Fred, surveying the fish. 'That fish looks like a 10-pounder. It ought to be a 10-pounder. Another week or two in the lake and it would have been a 10-pounder. And it's worth a bottle of whisky.'

There was gravel on the garden paths at the back of the Lodge. Fred seized a small garden trowel and rammed a decent quantity of gravel down the gullet of the dead fish.

47

Later that morning he departed in his truck and displayed the fish in the private bar of the Terraces Hotel. Johnny Sheehan himself officiated at the weighing ceremony, stuttering excitedly as was his habit.

'T-t-ten p-p-pounds and a b-b-bit,' he said. 'Wh-wh-what's your b-b-brand?'

Fred arrived back with the bottle intact, and we dealt with it faithfully that evening.

Johnny was not really the loser. Most of us used to keep him reasonably supplied with fish. It is illegal in New Zealand to sell trout. It cannot even appear on a hotel menu, although a hotel is permitted to cook trout caught by a guest and to serve it to the guest and to anyone else with whom the guest may wish to share his bounty. But in Johnny's day, while the sale of trout was even then illegal, it could appear on a hotel menu provided it had been caught by the proprietor or was a genuine gift.

Fred Fletcher operated a well-appointed smokehouse, but he used to clean his fish before smoking at a concrete step on the bank of the Mangamutu creek just outside the back door of the Lodge. Alongside the step was a battery of wires, each individually labelled, on which guests would hang in the creek the fish that they wanted to be smoked. In addition, there was Johnny's own special wire on which most of us would hang fish surplus to our own requirements or judged unsuitable for smoking. Johnny obtained a fairly regular supply, and the guests at the old Terraces Hotel were able to eat trout with most meals. The only trouble was that Johnny did not confine his collections to his own special wire. If there were fish on the other wires, he considered them fair game. Whenever his car was seen approaching the Lodge, one or other of us would hurriedly remove all fish from the private wires and take them to the sanctuary of the smokehouse.

Fred's fish-cleaning sessions often coincided with our

drinks before dinner. On a mild evening we would take our drinks out to the back garden, with an extra supply for Fred who imbibed happily while he stood in the creek in waders, gutting and splitting the fish. It was always a companionable interlude.

Dorothy and Ian Parsons were with us on one such occasion. They were Waitahanui regulars in those days, and the best of good company. Fred disliked the look of one of Dorothy's fish that he had just removed from the wire. He slit it open, gutted it, gave it another cursory inspection and then tossed it over his shoulder into the creek.

'Not worth smoking,' he declared. 'It'd look and taste like corrugated cardboard, only not as nice.'

Dorothy accepted the judgment without protest, and we finished our drinks and went to dinner. An hour or so later, several of us, Dorothy and Ian included, proceeded to the Rip for the night fishing session. It was a good, strong-flowing Rip, with ample room for all the dozen rods operating. In the dark, Dorothy took up station toward the left hand edge of the current, and very soon announced with delight that she had hooked a fish. In accordance with the unwritten rules, she moved across current to her right, passing her line over the heads of the other fishermen and confiding that her fish seemed to be behaving in a most peculiar fashion. She moved off into slack water and then back toward the beach, her line still taut. Once ashore, she reeled to get the fish out of the current and it came to the beach without the semblance of a fight. Dorothy shone her torch on it. Not only was the fish foul-hooked under one of its gill covers, but it was also slit from vent to gills and expertly gutted. It was the same fish that Fred had dis-carded a few hours earlier.

Much banter was directed at Dorothy when she gave us the facts on rejoining the Picket Fence. Not long after the banter switched to me. I felt a good, solid pull on my line and immediately struck what I took to be a heavy fish. It moved off down the current, not with any mad rush, but with a strange sort of zig-zag motion. I tightened on it, moved down the row of fishermen and, from the slack water, tried to coax it out of the current.

The fish seemed reluctant to move and, as I was fishing with light gear, I did not care to put too much pressure on it. Slowly I moved back to the beach, still yielding line, and then walked along to my right, hoping to coax the fish into quieter water. After what seemed to be an interminable period, the zig-zag motion ceased. I had the fish out of the current, but it still opposed a stubborn weight to my reeling.

The line came back slowly, but at long last a peculiar shape appeared on the wet sand at the water's edge. The beam of my torch revealed the horrible truth. I had hooked, played and landed an empty jam tin.

For years afterwards my Maori friends who were present would never let me forget about it. Old Harry Tahau would recall the incident at the slightest provocation. 'What was the jam?' he would always ask, 'Strawberry or plum and apple?'

Our Maori friends did much to enliven the fishing for us. Although they had handed over the fishing rights to the Government, they still owned a good deal of the land round the lake and rivers, and they retained a strong sense of property. But they were fishermen themselves and very few conflicts of interest arose between them and the holiday anglers who invaded their territory.

We all used to enjoy our good-natured exchanges with Hoppy Wall, one of the chief local guardians of Maori rights and privileges. Hoppy was a short, stocky Maori, lame in one leg and with other physical disabilities. And he was a considerable fisherman. Not until very late in life did he own a pair of waders. He would arrive on the beach at the Rip, change into swimming shorts or a tattered pair of trousers and then limp into the water to take his place in the line of fishermen.

On one occasion during his pre-wader days, Hoppy was moved to complain loudly and bitterly about the injustice of things in general. The river was flowing almost straight out into the lake and those of us who were fishing the Rip had to wade fairly deep to cover the water beyond a very steep ledge. Hoppy complained that it was unfair. We were all in deep waders, and we all stood about six feet or more, and how could the poor Maori, with no waders and no physical height, hope to compete? Too many pakeha fishermen, that was the trouble. They were all too tall and they all had enough money to buy waders, and the poor old Maori just didn't stand a chance. By this time Hoppy was wading about chin deep, casting away industriously and still lamenting.

The next day Hoppy appeared at the beach during the forenoon mounted on his ageing and mournful piebald horse. He surveyed the scene for a while in lordly fashion and then urged his horse into the water, bringing it finally to a halt in the middle of the line of fishermen. There, from his precarious seat in a rather decrepit saddle, he proceeded to cast out into the Rip.

'You see,' said Hoppy, 'I brought my waders.'

He even managed to hook a fish from his equestrian eminence, to move his horse sedately down the line of fishermen and back to the beach, and then to play the fish from the saddle until he finally decided to dismount and land it. Jock Howie immediately nominated Hoppy to be Colonel-in-Chief of the Waitahanui Light Horse, and Hoppy, having demonstrated his point, resumed his normal wading.

The Rip in those days provided the chief centre of angling activity. Comparatively few rods fished the river, although a fresh westerly and rough water at the river mouth would soon persuade fishermen to go venturing upstream; and from March onward, too, after the spawning runs had started, the pools and reaches on the last mile or so of river would receive attention.

It is a lovely river, the Waitahanui, and it was lovely even in the days of awkward access and barely discernible tracks. Very few anglers ever fished it above a pool known as the Crescent, although some of us were introduced by our Maori friends to neighbouring water which rarely saw an artificial fly. From the Crescent to the Rip would represent a twisting river distance of a couple of miles, more or less—but certainly much less if one knew the tracks. Over that river distance it was possible to fish a dozen obvious pools and at least half a dozen open reaches, and, as there seldom seemed to be more than about a dozen rods on the river, the water was never crowded.

After the war angling pressure increased, at first gradually and then explosively. About that time a number of us who fished regularly at Waitahanui decided to form a local angling association and one of our first tasks was to open up tracks to water further upstream and even to bridge the river at several points.

As the years went by, car tracks gradually took shape. They were rudimentary at first, little more than breaks through the prevailing growth of manuka, but gradually they were widened, cleared and even graded after a fashion, so that today it is possible to drive about three miles up the river valley—much more by actual river distance—and to do so in relative comfort and without damage to the paint-work of the car. But in the early stages of our river development nobody ever thought of driving up the track in anything but a light truck. A Bren gun carrier would have proved even more suitable.

River expeditions back in the late 40s and early 50s were

often all-day affairs. Either singly or in small groups, we would leave the Lodge after breakfast, generally in thigh boots to avoid the fatigue of a long hike in deep waders. Often we would organise transport by car for part of the way, dump our lunch haversacks and then continue for another mile or two along narrow foot tracks, getting occasional glimpses of the river as it wound its way through rough scrub country.

Those days on the river when you had to tramp for your fishing and work for your fish probably brought a greater sense of fulfilment than anything now experienced under conditions of easier access. You could head, for example, straight for the Gordon Williams Pool in the reasonably confident hope of having it to yourself. The pool at that time marked the upper limit of moderately accessible water, and it was and still is a joy to fish. You reached the pool by negotiating a couple of rickety foot bridges, first from left bank to right and then, at the pool itself, from right to left. The lower of the two bridges still stands. The upper bridge has been rendered superfluous by improved upstream access.

On its course northward from its source to the lake, the Waitahanui carves its pumice bed through exotic forest plantations and open basins of scrub and tussock, flanked by high pumice cliffs. Just above the Gordon Williams Pool one such basin narrows at its northern extremity and the river swings almost due west to flow headlong toward the southern escarpment before it swings right again on its northward course. There, just above the bend, lies the pool itself. On the run into the pool the river cascades merrily down a fairly narrow course, but it can be easily waded from a sandy ledge on the left bank. The water surges against your waders as you take your midstream stand about knee deep, and the whole prospect offers an invitation to fish for the sheer joy of fishing.

Immediately in front of you a diagonal lip shows where the river deepens into the pool proper. Downstream and to the left, part of the current reverses into a smooth backwater. Where the river takes its right-hand turn a little, rocky islet divides the stream. Immediately ahead the pumice cliffs rise almost sheer for 200 ft or more, clothed for some distance in tall white manuka, and then exposing weathered faces of pumice in the most incredible range of colours—rose, pink, yellow and buff.

Some years ago I arranged for a photographer from my staff to take several colour transparencies of the pool and its surroundings. When the films were reproduced as coloured illustrations, the blockmakers carefully toned down the colours in the high cliffs. The film colouring, they said, was just too extravagant to be true. In point of fact, the transparencies were accurate, the reproductions an understatement. The colours that sunlight can reveal in the pumice crags almost vibrate.

There, in the Gordon Williams Pool, it is a temptation to fish on indefinitely. If no fish are taking, you can walk ashore, climb a track to a slight eminence above the backwater and from that point of vantage survey the holding water and the lies. If a run is on, the chances are that you will spot half a dozen or more massive fish, pausing in their upstream migration. You could try them with another fly, perhaps, but an extended river expedition on foot seldom permitted too prolonged a concentration on a single and remote pool.

You would move on, possibly fishing two or three difficult lies on the way, to Butler's Bend, with its diagonal flow of current and the prospect of a fight with a fish in strong water. Two of us, a visiting Scotsman and myself, made such a downstream expedition some years ago. We took a fish apiece from the upper water—mine from the Gordon Williams Pool and Jock's from Butler's Bend—and then we divided the river between us, Jock crossing the little swing bridge to fish down from the left bank, while I took the track down the right bank. In this fashion we were fishing alternate pools, with neither of us covering the same water. We planned to meet at the next crossing, the Totara Bridge Pool, where we had dumped our lunch hamper from Ian Logan's truck on our way up the river.

It was a late lunch when we finally got round to it. We had each fished four different pools on our separate ways downstream. Jock proudly exhibited a bright 5-pounder that he had taken after a prolonged scrap in the turbulent water of the Pig Pool. I bemoaned the loss of a fish that I hooked near the tail of Murphy's Ruin, and that ran down into a narrow, overgrown gut where the water was too deep and swift to follow. But the autumn sunshine was warm, the bottles of beer that we had left anchored in the river by the bridge were deliciously chilled and a generous assortment of sandwiches vanished in a few ravenous minutes. Then came Jock's moment of the day. I produced the thermette to brew up for a pot of tea, and Jock sat spellbound.

The thermette, as far as I know, is a piece of outdoor equipment peculiar to New Zealand, simple but amazingly efficient. It consists of a short, cylindrical metal base that serves as a firebox, into which fits a taller, cylindrical water jacket which also serves as a chimney. In scrub country there is never any difficulty in finding ample twigs, sticks and dry wood for fuel. Once a decent fire is glowing in the miniature furnace base, you simply fill the water jacket from the river, fit it into position on the base and then feed the fire down the funnel. A quart or so of water comes to the boil in a matter of minutes, aromatic manuka smoke puffs out of the water jacket chimney and the whole contraption offers adequate safeguards against any incipient bushfire.

Jock was lost in admiration. Even after I had brewed the tea, he insisted on refilling and refuelling the thermette, and there he sat, enchanted by the bubbling sound, the drift of smoke and the small plume of steam. Where could he get a few of these gadgets to take back with him to Scotland?

I told him that they were on sale in practically every hardware shop, and later he wrote to me, saying that before his departure from Auckland he had bought three—one for himself, one for an angling companion in Scotland and one to serve as a model for some interested manufacturer to supply the Scottish market.

We left our lunch gear, including the admired thermette, having arranged with Ian Logan that he would collect it with his truck, and we proceeded to fish our way home. From the Totara Bridge downstream the river becomes rather less overgrown, with open pools and reaches occurring every hundred yards or so. Most of the water is best fishable from the left bank, and two rods can proceed down the river leapfrog fashion, with an ample choice of pools and an interesting selection of local hazards. The day was getting older, but the river still chuckled and sang, the bellbirds called to one another as they flitted invisibly through the surrounding manuka and the tangy smell of the bush filled the air. The dead flower stems of native flax thrust upward like spears from the tall green leaves, some residual gold bloomed on broom and lupins, ripe blackberries were there for the picking and an occasional clump of pines, stand of poplars or venerable bluegum rose from the wild undergrowth. That was and still is the charm of the river valley— an open place, yet with more than a touch of the primitive. You thought then, and you still think, that the river, as it winds and thrusts its way through the rough landscape, both welcomes the wild fish that run into it and yet consents to offer a share of them to predatory man.

Jock lingered for some time at the Crescent after taking

a lively fish from its attractive water where the river sweeps down into a deep pool beneath a low pumice cliff and then pours out abruptly to the left. Eventually he followed me downstream just in time to see me land a respectable fish from my favourite Flaxbush Pool. I had forded the river twice, following the fish downstream, so we retraced our steps that I might recover my earlier catch from its repository at the head of the Flaxbush. There Jock immediately became interested in a small hole that very few of the regulars ever fish. His angler's eye spotted a diagonal swing in the current over toward the right bank where a darker colour tone proclaimed deeper water.

'A fish ought to be lying there,' said Jock, and sure enough one was. He hit it at his very first cast, held it firmly within the narrow limits of the pool and finally backed his way to the bank. Once there, his room for manoeuvre was restricted to the narrow gap in the manuka leading back to the main track. Jock played his fish until he had it surfaced on a short line, and then he literally ran in reverse through the cleared access way. He actually reached the main track before the fish flapped desperately on the bank.

Years later I attempted the same Caledonian technique on the Brodhead, a pleasant little river in Eastern Pennsylvania where I have frequently fished as the guest of American friends. On this occasion I had hooked a fish near the end of a fairly long run, with awkward bank conditions downstream. It was a good fish for the Brodhead, where a 2-pounder calls for admiration, and rather than risk dragging it back against the current, I decided to emulate Jock's run astern. I had hardly gathered speed when my left heel hit a boulder. Down I went flat on my behind, and the fly was torn violently from the mouth of the trout to land in the surrounding vegetation.

But back to our day on the Waitahanui. On our downstream journey I managed to coax a fish out of the lower water of the Parade, a couple of hundred yards away from the scene of Jock's run astern, and, as the sun dipped behind the tall pines, we fished our way down to the Poi Pool beat, where Ian Logan discovered us, still casting hopefully, and persuaded us back to his truck with the suggestion that there might just be time for a couple of drinks before dinner. So back we went to the Lodge with our joint bag of seven fish and with Jock singing the praises of the river in language that might have come straight from Burns or Walter Scott. And after drinks and a substantial dinner we summoned up energy enough for a final hour at the Rip which yielded us a fish apiece to put the seal on an active and happy day.

Nine fish for two rods in about ten fishing hours did not constitute a remarkable bag. The daily rod limit at that time was six fish and neither of us achieved it, although Jock remained hopeful that his final cast at the Rip on the stroke of eleven o'clock would bring him his limit fish. What stayed in my mind as I stretched out finally in bed was the quality of the day—bright sunshine, clean air, the tangy bush scents, the music of the running river, the sense of anticipation at every pool, the exhilaration as each succeeding fish took the fly. The final hour at the Rip, too; the night dark velvet and mild, the stars like jewels, the lake calm and quiet except for the plash of the current where the urgent flow of the river met its placid barrier, the occasional scream of a reel, the sudden surge of a fighting fish.

The really Golden Past of the Waitahanui, as with all other Taupo waters, fell within the first decade of the present century, just after Rainbow trout had been successfully established in the fishery. It was revived briefly in the 1920s, following an intensive campaign of netting to reduce a trout population that had outgrown its indigenous food supplies. The records of the early years are at best fragmentary, but there is in existence the diary of an English angler named King-Webster who fished at Taupo in 1908 and 1909.

Those were the days when transport was primitive. King-Webster travelled from Rotorua to Taupo by horse-drawn coach. 'The drive was 56 miles and we changed horses three times. The roads are very bad and we only averaged six miles an hour.' It is still about 56 miles from Rotorua to Taupo, but the journey by car today takes little more than an hour.

King-Webster's objective was the Tongariro River, at the southern end of the lake, but in 1908 road access between Taupo and Tokaanu was non-existent. The journey had to be made by small steamer down the full length of a lake often subject to quite considerable storms. Under good conditions, the trip took about three hours. King-Webster fished triumphantly, at times almost incredulously, on the Tongariro, taking most of his fish on spinning tackle until he discovered for himself that it was possible to take them on the wet fly, provided that he could make the fly swim deep enough. Fish running into double-figure weight were common, and his best was one of 19 lb.

To fish the Waitahanui, King-Webster had to make the return steamer trip down the lake from Tokaanu to Taupo, spend a night at Taupo and then travel the eight miles to the river by horsedrawn brake over rutted pumice tracks. For three days he lived in what must have been an exceed-ingly rough and ready camp. 'There were no towels, no blankets or rugs, and everything was dirty. I had to sleep in my clothes and a rug which I fortunately brought with me.'

Yet in those three days King-Webster took seventeen fish with a total weight of 166 lb. His best was a 14 lb Rainbow, taken in the little Mangamutu stream which flows parallel with the lower reaches of the Waitahanui, but in the

opposite direction, before it joins the main river at Dela-
tour's Pool.

From that same water, a creek that annually attracts an
incredible run of spawning fish, legend has it that some
enterprising Maori took the heaviest Rainbow ever landed
at Taupo and reputed to weigh 37½ lb. Even bigger Brown
trout were caught at Taupo during the early years. Here
again official records are not available for checking, but the
older Maoris insist that a monster landed at the southern
end of the lake weighed 51½ lb.

At the age of five years, I caught my first trout on a
pleasant little river in South Canterbury near a village with
the appropriate name of Pleasant Point. Taupo at that time
was not even a name to me, but its really legendary fishing
was already over. Nor did I personally experience the brief
revival of the 1920s when, for a couple of seasons, certain
anglers contemptuously returned to the water any fish under
10 lb in weight. My Taupo fishing has proceeded happily
since the mid-1930s, and the Golden Past for me is not so
much a period of huge fish as a span of years during which
the rivers were less crowded, the fish seemingly more
plentiful and the fishermen infinitely more punctilious in
their regard for the ethics of the sport.

Most of my early mentors are gone now, Maori as well
as pakeha. In particular, I miss the older Maoris. They were
superb fishermen, as, indeed, some of their sons and grandsons still are today. I place a Maori of my generation as the
finest natural fisherman I have ever seen. But the elders were
men of great natural dignity, proud of their race, happy in
their simple rural life, great tellers of tales once their confidence was gained, and on the water the best of good
companions. I would surrender many of my present
pleasures for one day at the Rip or on the river in the
company of Awhi Northcroft, Harry Tahau and Kapua. All
I can say is that some of their example rests with me in the

tying of fly to cast, the visual timing of the back cast in a tricky wind, an eye for where the fish may lie in a pool, odd scraps of watercraft and weather wisdom.

For most fishermen, as they grow older, the past seems always golden, but they are no longer fishermen once they fail to hear the call of the running trout.

III

PRESENT PLEASURES

Even if old fishermen recall nostalgically the years in which the rivers were less crowded and the fish seemingly more plentiful, many of us can still rejoice in our present pleasures and count ourselves lucky that we still have the ability to cast a reasonably long line and to handle a fighting fish. I do not fish much at night nowadays, but, except in winter, I love the dawn parade and the magic of the two fishing hours before breakfast.

In our antipodean spring and early summer, it is broad daylight at five o'clock in the morning. Indeed, the first light is already starting to brighten the sky if I roll out of bed at four o'clock to sniff the weather. A fresh westerly makes the Waitahanui Rip unfishable, and our home is sheltered from this particular wind. But certain tall trees serve as weather vanes and there is always the voice of the lake. If the voice rises above a murmur in our quiet bay, I simply go back to bed and hope that the wind will drop later in the day. Generally, however, the dawn is peaceful and the wind, if westerly weather is forecast, freshens later in the day.

The important thing is to be out at Waitahanui and into waders before five o'clock, the legal hour at which fishing can be resumed after the retreat at eleven o'clock on the preceding night. You may find another car or two parked at the roadside and you may find a few other fishermen standing on the beach, awaiting the magic hour. But, except at holiday times, the Rip is seldom crowded in the early mornings. Often I wade in at five o'clock with the whole expanse of water to myself—although seldom for more than half an hour.

It is the first cast of the early morning that always has me on tenterhooks. For six hours the water has been completely undisturbed, and the trout habitually cruise inshore during the hours of darkness in quest of food. Will they still be there, or will they have moved out into deeper water? Occasionally you will see them porpoising along the edge of the current as it surges into the lake, and your fingers tighten on the cork grip of your rod.

More often than not, a few fish take within the first few minutes. They may continue taking for an hour or more. But, as the season progresses and you start fishing in the dark, the early take seems to be confined to the old cruising fish, but with a period of much greater activity just as the sun starts to rise. Trout generally seem responsive to a change of light.

Not so very long ago, in the first summer of our permanent Taupo residence, I took the young man who is now my stepson-in-law to the Waitahanui Rip for the dawn parade. David had not done very much fly fishing, but he knew how to handle a rod and line and I had briefed him on the Waitahanui techniques. Three or four other rods accompanied us as we waded in off the beach in the dim early light before sunrise. As luck would have it, I struck a fish first cast. It dashed off to the left out of the current and into still water, and I had a long wade back to the sandspit that separates the final reach of the river from the lake.

Finally I beached, killed and buried my fish, but as I waded back toward the Rip, with the light growing stronger, I noticed David some distance behind the row of casting fishermen. 'What the devil,' I thought, 'is he doing there?' Then I saw his rod arched and a fish jumping about thirty yards in front of him. He had hooked it, he told me, just after I had hooked my fish, but he was nervous about moving down the Rip and passing his line over the heads of the fishermen on his right.

'Back toward the beach,' I instructed him. 'Don't reel. Just walk and the fish will probably come with you. And when you get him behind the other rods, move down the beach to your right and play him out.'

I was determined that David should land his fish unaided. Clearly it was well hooked, and the spare rod and line with which I had equipped him were adequate for the task. He moved backward and to his right, but seemed reluctant to leave the water. I yelled to him to get on the beach where he would have greater freedom of movement. Eventually he did so and continued to play his fish with extreme care until some time later the thud of a lump of pumice on the head of the fish signalled the last rites and the end of the battle.

David rejoined me at the Rip with the light of triumph in his eyes but too excited to speak. We fished on until seven o'clock, but ours were the only two fish landed that early morning. Occasional rises out beyond the current indicated that the fish had sought deeper water. We waded ashore and recovered our fish from their separate graves, and they looked like a pigeon pair, bright silver and beautifully shaped. At the car I produced my 'de-liar', combined spring balance and metal measuring tape. The two fish were identical in weight at 6½ lb, but David's was 22 in. in length and mine 23 in. On condition factor, David claimed the better fish. His day was made.

A few months later David and my stepdaughter Jan were married. On his first post-nuptial birthday, David's present from his wife was a Hardy rod.

Once experienced, early mornings on Taupo waters become an abiding joy, both in reality and in remembered delight. Naturally, one chooses one's time. A hard, frosty morning brings with it no overpowering urge to leave the civilised comfort of an electric blanket. The sound of waves on the beach likewise prescribes the extra hours in bed. But on a mild morning in late summer or early autumn the dawn hours make the day.

From late March onward, when the fish start to move into the rivers, dawn fishing can be a chancy business. The early mornings can prove distinctly chilly and the frosts seem to descend as the day starts to brighten. Under such conditions, Rip or river fishing offers few attractions, except for those hardy souls who muffle themselves against the cold. They often fare better in the lower reaches of the river than at the Rip, taking their share of the fish that have made a late entry from the lake and are still adjusting themselves to the strength of the current.

How long it takes a Rainbow to accustom itself to fast water after two years or more in still water, I do not know. The experts tell us that the sensory system of the trout is extraordinarily well developed and in all probability the adjustment is rapidly achieved. The marine biologists say that fish running from the lake lose their bright silver within forty-eight hours of entering a river. Yet in late autumn and early winter I have taken bright silver fish from the upper pools of the Waitahanui or the Tongariro—fish that must have travelled four or five miles of river distance against strong currents in less than forty-eight hours.

Over recent seasons, too, some change seems to have occurred in the running habits of the Taupo trout. They remain vulnerable in the lower reaches of the rivers, where they are heavily fished, but then, by all the evidence, they appear to ignore almost completely the known holding pools in which the running fish of earlier seasons were accustomed to gather energy for the next onslaught on the current.

Nobody can say for certain how many fish lie at any given time in a given stretch of river. Even with polaroid glasses, no fisherman could hope to conduct an accurate census. Yet times without number when we have had indisputable evidence of runs into the lower reaches, we find the higher pools apparently barren. At the same time, the fisheries officers, who make regular surveys of the actual spawning waters after the runs start, report these waters to be literally black with fish.

Whether the fish have been rendered line-shy in the lower reaches, or whether they have reacted physically to variations in water temperatures and pressures remains a matter of conjecture. Whatever is happening, the pattern of the runs could prove a useful subject for research. Electric fish counters are common enough these days and fairly accurate data could certainly be obtained by monitoring the runs at selected points over a suitable stretch of river. The information thus obtained would have to be correlated with temperature readings, both air and water, measurements of river flow and variations in lake levels. Then would come the physical task of trying to control and regulate the runs.

Differences between air and water temperatures could well prove the determining factor. Many of us have long believed that fishing is hardest when the air temperature is lower than the water temperature. The theory is that under such conditions the trout simply go to the bottom and remain more or less comatose. Could it be that they are spurred to sudden activity and that they charge upstream at a furious rate, ignoring all enticements offered to them on the way?

Speculation serves very little purpose in the absence of systematic research. Until the experts prove the point one way or another, I remain content to confine my winter river fishing to the hours when the sun is on the water. It is the comfortable way to fish, even if the trout themselves are not always wildly co-operative.

We have established earlier in this book a rough sort of Taupo angling calendar, based on the movement of the fish from and to the lake before and after spawning. It follows that, throughout the late spring, the summer and the early autumn, fly fishing is mostly confined to the zones of the river mouths, from which bait-casters, trollers and other hardware merchants are mercifully excluded. For nearly half the year, from late October to late March, the Taupo tributaries, in the main, hold few, if any, takeable fish.

An exception must be made in the case of the Tongariro River which, for some peculiar reason, seems to attract a late summer run of immature maiden fish. The run generally occurs in February and may extend over several weeks, depending on weather conditions and the height of the river. The fish, I think, are premature spawners, migrating from the lake before they are fully ripe to spawn. They seldom weigh more than $3\frac{1}{2}$ lb, but they are bright silver and full of fight.

Quite frequently in recent seasons, when the river mouth fishing in the northern sector of the lake has proved hard and unrewarding, I have taken visiting anglers to the Tongariro and put them into one or other of my favourite pools. On one such expedition, an American friend, well accustomed to handling Rainbows in fast water, worked twice down the length of the superb Major Jones Pool. He landed and killed four excellent fish, lost five which he had hooked and played much more than momentarily and missed quite a number on the strike. To him, the $3\frac{1}{2}$-pounders were notable fish and the day's fishing an absolute joy. His cup was full when, on the following evening at the Waitahanui Rip, he landed a 6-pounder.

The Tongariro is the best part of an hour's drive from my home, and I don't fish it as often as I should. So, until the major runs start, the bulk of my fishing from November to April is at the Waitahanui Rip. Nor do I confine myself to the early mornings. The noonday sessions yield splendid sport when, under favourable conditions, the fish seem to come suddenly and explosively on the take.

You can wade in from the roadside beach at the Rip and there may not be a single fish moving in or beyond the current. You cast across the Rip happily enough in the warm summer sunshine, occasionally changing flies in a hopeful and experimental fashion, and then suddenly, as the sun approaches its zenith, either you or one of your companions in the line of fishermen will hit a fish. Then the chances are that there will be a flurry of activity, with fish taking the fly swiftly and unexpectedly. Unless there has been a run of smelt, the trout seldom advertise their presence. They take deep, but quite often close up to the lip, catching you with a handful of retrieved line which you must free and tighten before you get your fish on the reel. It is splendid fishing when it occurs and quite often it has sent me home for a very late lunch.

Even in the broad, open waters of a lake like Taupo the trout seem to change station with the sun. On the eastern shores they tend to move out into deeper water as the sun climbs behind the hopeful row of mouth fishermen, but at the noonday height, with the absence of oblique shadows, they apparently move to accommodate themselves for the westering sun. Or perhaps it just happens to be their feeding hour and they move in toward the ledge where the pressure of the lake restrains the river current and where a well-stocked larder awaits them.

If the noonday strike comes up to expectations, the fish may not move far out into deeper water as the afternoon progresses. Thus, if I manage to collect a fish or two on the noonday strike, I am always tempted to take my rod and waders again in the late afternoon and drive back to the Rip for the sunset hour.

The cool of the evening seems to be a time of day sacred to trout fishermen anywhere and everywhere. At Taupo the sunset hour possesses its own special magic. We fish, most of us, from the eastern shores of the lake and on a clear day the sun slips toward the western hills in a blaze of glory. The glare across the wide expanse of lake is often dazzling in its intensity and, according to the flow of the current, you may find yourself casting directly into the rays of the setting sun. Sometimes you long for a passing cloud to dim the splendour and bring relief to strained eyes.

'The sun's rim dips.' Now is the magic hour, and yet it is completely unpredictable. On occasions the whole expanse of water adjacent to the Rip will suddenly become alive with fish. They will break surface in fantastic and lovely movement. Some will leap clear of the water and gleam incredibly refulgent in the sunset glow. They will move in and out of the current, snatching as they go at a well-cast fly. On another evening there may be no surface sign of fish whatsoever, yet they will be lying deep and feeding avidly. Honesty, nevertheless, compels the admission that there are many evenings when it does not matter a rap whether the fish are visible or invisible; they simply will not take. Not a fly in the box will arouse their interest—not even my dark rabbit skin version of the Claret and Mallard which is my standby for the sunset hour.

It is then that the patient and persistent fisherman bides his time until dark, for the night fishing at Taupo is generally the most productive of all. These days in my retirement I do not fish at nights nearly as much as I was used to do on my angling vacations of former years. Yet on occasions I find myself tempted, particularly on a calm, mild evening after a spell of westerly weather. For a westerly at the Waitahanui Rip forces the current to swing in a northerly direction, almost parallel with the lakeshore. Under such conditions the fishing need never be crowded and, provided you do not encounter a garrulous neighbour to right or left, you can be at peace with the world.

Night fishing brings with it its own magic, its own mystery. Some folk affect to despise it, claiming that when line and fly become invisible the whole art of casting must be surrendered to 'chuck-and-chance-it' methods, and that even the playing of a hooked fish loses its appeal because of the lack of visual awareness.

Most emphatically I disagree. Even on the darkest night at Taupo some faint luminosity remains in the velvet sky. There may or may not be a moon. If there is no cloud, the stars sparkle with an unbelievable brilliance. Once the eyes become accustomed to the dark, it is perfectly easy to discern the flow of the current which in any case carries its own soft music to the ear. With gear to which you are accustomed, it is a simple matter to judge the length of line that you must strip off the reel to cast smoothly and accurately across the current and swing your fly round in an arc for the slow, anticipatory retrieve.

You do not see your fish, but then even in daytime Rip fishing the fish that breaks surface is seldom the one that takes your fly. On a still night you can hear them, and that is part of the fascination of the whole process. An almighty splash out beyond the current and you immediately wonder what sized fish it was that created such a disturbance. You will persuade yourself that it was a monster and subconsciously you will try to will it within the orbit of your fly.

The strike of the Taupo Rainbow at night defies prediction. Sometimes there will be a quiet tightening of the line as if a cruising fish had almost casually taken the fly. At other times the rod is almost jerked from your hand, the reel makes instant music and the line disappears into the void as the trout makes its first frantic run. After that it is largely a matter of experience, playing the fish to get it back on a reasonably short line, coaxing it across the current and then carrying the battle to it in quieter water until finally you see the gleam of silver and ease the fish of mystery onto the wet sand.

By some optical illusion, a Rainbow beached at night always seems to be bigger, brighter and better-proportioned than a comparable fish landed in daylight. More often than not, fancy proves to be fact. The largest Rainbows, and certainly the largest Browns, seem to be caught at night, but that is simply in accordance with the feeding habits of the fish which normally wait for darkness before they make their hungry raids into the shallows. You strike a fish, you do battle with it to the best of your ability and you rarely know what you are about to achieve until the ultimate moment of triumph.

River fishing at night calls for a rather more adventurous spirit. In most Taupo waters it is necessary to wade to cover the known lies, and most fishermen like to see where they are going. I have fished several Taupo rivers and streams at night, but on all of them I have restricted myself to pools that I know intimately and in which I am not likely to be tempted to any hazardous indiscretions in playing or following a hooked fish.

Morning, noon or night, the present pleasures of Taupo fishing retain many of the splendours of the Golden Past. The magnificent expanse of the lake still delights the eye. The rivers and streams supply it joyously and generously with their abundant waters. Human habitations multiply with every passing year, but wide stretches of lakeshore and river valley remain more or less as Nature made them, and there are those of us who do all we can, in our various ways, to preserve as far as possible an environment that would be ruined if it were ever to become urbanised and over-developed.

Man, not Nature, is the enemy. Sooner, rather than later, every true trout fisherman becomes at heart a conservationist, and we can examine later in some detail the efforts of the conservationists to preserve and protect the lake and its environs against ill-conceived intrusions. Unfortunately, however, physical interference with the environment does not constitute the only threat to our present pleasures. Certain angling techniques and practices have developed to make a mockery of the Golden Past.

A few years ago the greatest weight of Taupo fish—probably seventy-five per cent of an annual harvest in excess of 500 tons—used to be taken by fly fishermen at the river mouths and in the rivers, even with a closed season enforced for five months of the year. Then came the aquatic invasion. Boats of varying shapes and sizes became fashionable and popular. They could be transported for long distances on trailers and launched at any convenient spot round the perimeter of the lake.

Only commercial hire launches are licensed and it is difficult at any time to calculate the numerical strength of the armada of pleasure craft on Taupo waters at weekends and during the holiday seasons. Sample checks are made from time to time, and one such boat census in January, 1973, disclosed the presence of more than 2,400 boats actually on the lake during the hours of daylight on one Sunday.

The boating craze more or less coincided with a managerial decision to abandon the closed season and to permit fishing on all Taupo waters, except for defined spawning areas, all the year round. At the same time, earlier restrictions on the type of tackle that could be used for trolling were substantially eased. Heavy sinking lines with metal cores, previously banned, suddenly became legal. The managerial aim was to step up the harvest of fish so that the trout population of the lake might be kept more in balance with the available food supply.

A change in the angling pattern immediately occurred. Whereas earlier the bulk of the annual catch went to fly fishermen at the river mouths and in the rivers, nowadays about seventy-five per cent of the trout harvested over the whole district are taken by trollers on the lake. To make matters worse, a high proportion of the boat catch consists of immature, two-year-old fish. At that age the average Taupo Rainbow is well above the legal size limit of 14 in., and can therefore be killed and taken legitimately by the boat fisherman. It stands to reason that the number of mature fish congregating in season round the river mouths and subsequently making their spawning runs into the rivers is being appreciably reduced.

The management authorities maintain that they are watching the position carefully. They hold that winter fishing and increased pressure by the trollers have resulted in a desirable culling of the stock, with a resultant improvement in the average weight, length and condition factor of the trout that run to spawn. They produce statistics to support their case and they attribute seasonal variations mainly to climatic conditions.

For instance, during one recent winter the Taupo rainfall was substantially below normal. There was a complete absence of natural flooding in the spawning tributaries and the survival rate of alevins and fingerlings hatched during that particular winter was exceptionally high. The authorities were worried. They had been considering the re-imposition of earlier restrictions, but came to the conclusion that, if they were arbitrarily to reduce the angling harvest, they might raise the trout population, at least temporarily, beyond the capacity of the lake to provide adequate food supplies. So the daily bag limit remained unaltered and the boat fishers continued to troll deep for a high proportion of immature fish.

Then Nature took a hand—in unfortunate combination with man. As a result of sudden increases in the demand for hydro-electric power, the allegedly controlled lake level during the following year went up and down in a bewildering and completely unnatural fashion. Smelt, the principal forage fish for the trout, suffered a phenomenally poor spawning season. They spawn prolifically, these little silvery fish, on the shores of the lake, and sudden variations in lake levels either fatally expose or equally fatally submerge millions of smelt ova before hatching occurs.

The combination of circumstances produced the inevitable results. An unusually high crop of young trout was present in the lake; a year's food supply was reduced below normal. In the next succeeding year the average weight and condition factor of the trout taken throughout the Taupo fishery showed a marked decline. But the management folk were satisfied that, if they had not condoned the continued taking of young fish by the trollers, the decline would have proved even more pronounced. Once again, it was a question of keeping the trout population and the natural food supply in some sort of balance.

After this one unhappy experience, conditions swiftly returned more or less to normal. Fortunately, the agricultural scientists played some part in the restoration. At their urgent behest, and for reasons entirely unconnected with the trout fishery, the Government had imposed a ban on certain insecticides widely used on farm lands throughout the Taupo district. As if by magic, a wealth of trout food suddenly descended on Taupo waters—unprecedented swarms of the native green beetle.

The green beetle is an attractive little creature, common in most parts of New Zealand. It appears in its greatest numbers during late spring and early summer, at the height of the smelt spawning season. Manuka scrub and other lakeside and riverside vegetation house whole colonies of the beetle, and since the spring of 1971 the colonies, freed from the lethal pesticides, have proliferated amazingly. Spring winds at Taupo can be fairly gusty and periodically they sweep the green beetle colonies from the abundant manuka and scatter them on lake and river. The green beetle has always been a favourite trout food, but when the beetle fall normally occurred in the back country most of the mature fish were out of the rivers and back in the lake. Succeeding generations of young trout have habitually gorged themselves on the green beetle falls in the rivers, but their elders, maturing or recovering in the lake, have had access to the supplementary diet only when the spring winds happened to scatter green beetle colonies in certain favoured lakeside areas.

The liberation from pesticides brought about a change in the established pattern. To a greater extent than ever before, the green beetle were scattered on the waters of the lake, close inshore, and the trout soon discovered them. A few anglers likewise chanced on areas where there had been heavy falls, and those who had the good sense to fish an imitation beetle on the surface took limit bags. But the green beetle fall in any particular area invariably occurred as the result of an offshore wind, and the zones of heaviest lakeside vegetation are not always easily accessible to the fly fisher. The real significance of the occurrence lay in the fact that,

75

while the trout were feasting royally on the green beetle, they were largely ignoring the shoaling and spawning smelt. The little fish welcomed the brief immunity, and the Wildlife people say that their numbers have increased enormously, although their spawning habits remain as unpredictable as ever.

The Waitahanui Rip is a feeding area and a pre-spawning assembly area for the trout, but it is not an area where one can expect a fall of green beetle. Yet from 1971 to 1974, in the late spring and early summer months, the fish that I took and killed at the Rip, on being opened up for cleaning, revealed stomach contents almost exclusively of green beetle. The fish were all taken on standard Taupo patterns of sunk fly. The conclusion I came to was that some trout at least, after a magnificent hors d'oeuvre course of green beetle, went cruising in search of a main course of smelt, or bully, or koura (the freshwater crayfish) and in doing so became vulnerable to the fly fisherman still angling for them by traditional methods.

One thing, I think, is certain: If the green beetle falls maintain their recent prolific nature, anglers will be encouraged to search for them, exploring suitable stretches of lakeshore under favourable weather conditions and, when they find the trout on the feed, enjoying a form of dry fly fishing that must be experienced to be believed. Generally it is inshore fishing and only short casting is necessary. A floating line, a greased cast and an imitation beetle designed to ride the water—these are the essentials. The technique is to fish up-wind or cross-wind if possible, allowing the artificial beetle to drift and jobble with the gentle wave action. And if the trout are active the fly will not drift or jobble for long.

Unfortunately, we cannot guarantee that natural causes, aided by occasional accidents of human benevolence, will always prevail over the misdirected activities of man. The smelt are still at the mercy of variable lake levels, artificially induced. The green beetle at any time may fall victim to new chemical insecticides approved by the agricultural scientists as being harmless to human beings. Meanwhile the lead-line troller will continue to take his harvest of immature trout from deep water, unless and until it is determined officially that he is getting more than his fair share. At the same time, so-called fly fishermen will explore and exploit devious ways of angling for trout in fly water simply to redress the balance at present in favour of the trollers.

The Golden Past of Taupo belonged to men who abided scrupulously by the rules, written and unwritten, in their fishing for trout. Our Present Pleasures are to some extent at the mercy not only of engineers and soil scientists and water polluters but also of a certain breed of fish-hungry individual who seeks loopholes in the rules and who, in fact, interprets the rules to suit himself.

Taupo waters are almost without exception open waters —an inestimable privilege for anyone who buys a licence and who is happy to fish, whether in waders or from a boat, in accordance with the regulations as they may be varied and adjusted from time to time. Under those regulations, all the rivers and defined zones round the river mouths, as well as certain other gazetted areas, are reserved for fishing with artificial fly only. Argument arises nowadays when one attempts to define what is fly fishing and what is not.

I have already described the lamentable state of affairs that developed on the famous Lupin Stretch of the Waitahanui River, immediately upstream from the lake. Platoons of so-called fly fishermen paraded at intervals in line abreast across the current, few of them bothering to cast except at rare intervals, but all of them paying out line and retrieving in an endeavour to hook fish newly entered into the river and still adjusting themselves to strong water. Trolling at the halt, I have called it, and I know of no more polite terms in which to describe a technique which seems to me to defy all the accepted principles of fly fishing. The practitioners have always argued that they are there to take fish and that they achieve their purpose; but the fish that they do not take must inevitably be rendered line-shy and probably remain in that highly nervous condition until they reach the closed waters of the spawning redds.

Opinions may differ on whether or not the practice is sportsmanlike or legal, but it has not been confined to one stretch of the Waitahanui. It has invaded some of the majestic pools of the Tongariro where it has become customary for certain anglers to position themselves in a pool above a known lie and then, on a long line, to swim a fly up and down the current through the fish. Like their Waitahanui counterparts, they rarely cast, except possibly after changing a fly. They monopolise whole stretches of water, either until they take their limit of fish or until they give up through sheer boredom.

Their number is swollen by the devotees of the shooting head on monofilament. The disciples of this particular cult also tend to become stationary anglers, combing the water with their flies from the exceptional length of cast that they can achieve with their new-fangled tackle. They lose a lot of flies on a boulder-bedded river like the Tongariro, which is hardly more than poetic justice, but they also deny other anglers the legitimate use of open water.

The shooting head on monofilament is unquestionably a most useful device for a certain type of fisherman and for a certain type of fishing. The gear enables the person using it virtually to employ bait-casting techniques with a fly rod. In water reserved for artificial fly only, bait-casting is banned, and I see no reason why the shooting head on monofilament should not likewise be banned on fly water.

On unrestricted open water I should regard it as perfectly permissible.

The experts with shooting head on monofilament occasionally invade the Waitahanui Rip and other river mouths and take fish beyond the normal range of the average fly caster. When somebody protests that they are forcing the fish out into deeper water, they reply that they are not getting out much further than the chap with the double-handed rod, and anyway it's perfectly legal, so what the hell?

Mercifully, the shooting head brigade has not invaded the Taupo rivers other than the Tongariro. The pools on rivers like the Waitahanui and the Tauranga-Taupo can be covered adequately by anyone who is no more than moderately proficient with a fly rod and a standard type of fly line. Indeed, on most such water the shooting head would probably prove an embarrassment rather than an advantage.

The long-liners are nothing if not ingenious. One method of fishing which has become popular with some of them was developed, as far as I can judge, by a young Maori whom I first saw in operation at the Waitahanui Rip in 1969. It was the season of my partial disablement and I was fishing in company with seven other rods at a Rip which was running straight out into the lake at right angles to the beach. The young Maori appeared in the late forenoon, took up station on the left hand edge of the current and very soon was playing his first fish which broke water at a distance of about a hundred yards. He landed the fish and within minutes was into another which again surfaced far out into the lake.

In conversation with those who were fishing near him, the young Maori explained his technique. He was fishing with a wide drum reel of large diameter and with a heavy double taper sinking line of thirty-five yards. To the reel end of his casting line he had spliced four connected twenty-five-yard lengths of level floating line. He would cast his sinking line—which he could do quite competently —and when it had straightened in the current he would pay out any still left on the reel, following it with the whole hundred yards of floating line. Then he would retrieve by hand fifty yards or so of floating line before letting it drift out again with the current.

So it went on; and within three hours the young Maori had landed and killed eleven fish. Not one fish took within normal casting range, and not one other fisherman at the Rip during those three hours as much as touched a fish.

Among the fish-hungry, the method gained a number of adherents. During the following season I was fishing at the Rip one morning when another fisherman known casually to me came in on my right where there was no great strength of current. After his initial casts he started to pay out inordinate lengths of line and it was plain to see that he, too, was fishing with a generous yardage of floating line spliced to the back of his casting line. I must have regarded him with something approaching contempt, because he volunteered the rather shamefaced explanation that he was 'trying out a new method'.

I replied that the method wasn't altogether new and it certainly was not fly fishing. If he wanted to catch fish beyond casting distance, why didn't he buy or hire a boat and take up trolling?

That was the last time I saw this particular fisherman experimenting with the 'new method'. But others have adopted it and continue to cause endless trouble when their abominable floating lines are caught up by legitimate casters.

The young Maori who apparently originated the whole wretched practice also added his own refinements. He joined me at the Rip one early morning. The two of us had the water to ourselves and the long-liner felt encouraged to fish right in the centre of the current. On practically every cast I would pick up the floating section of his line. 'I'll free it,' he would call out, and would hurriedly do so.

Then, as luck would have it, I picked up his line when he must have been reeling in either to examine or change his fly, and not until I had dragged his cast and fly within viewing distance did he realise what had happened. Even more anxiously than before, he shouted that he would free the lines, but by that time I had observed beyond any possibility of error the presence of his additional secret weapon—a fair-sized lump of trout roe impaled on the hook of his fly.

I laughed out loud as the young Maori hastened to retrieve his forbidden bait. Possibly my laughter carried a rather sardonic tone, because the poacher, after floating his long line once more down the current, reeled in and left the water. It was the last occasion on which I saw him at Waitahanui. He may have left the district, or he may have thought it safer to confine his fishing to the hours of darkness.

Fishing, as we do, on open water at Taupo, we must be prepared to encounter all sorts of fishermen, some of them not too scrupulous about the methods that they employ. The long-liners fall into that unfortunate category. So, too, do another class whom I describe as the stock-whippers. They fish with more line off the reel than they can conceivably cast and, having achieved their maximum casting distance (generally rather inexpertly), they use the rod with a violent stockwhip action to throw the surplus line in huge coils across the current. It is not a legitimate mending of the cast to slow down the swing of the fly; it is simply an ill-mannered ploy to fish beyond casting range.

Much of the effort is not infrequently wasted. Any experienced fly fisherman knows that trout, particularly Rainbows, will take at times almost at your feet, provided that there has been no violent disturbance of the water. But no fish in its sober senses is going to approach within several rod lengths if huge coils of cordage are being splashed about indiscriminately. Most of the long-liners, whatever objectionable method they use, merely succeed in forcing the fish out still further from the shore, thus spoiling the prospects for those who cast cleanly and competently to cover the water where the trout would normally lie.

Under Taupo conditions the long-liner spoils the fishing most noticeably and most reprehensibly at the river mouths where custom hallows fishing in groups. But the same gentry also operate on the larger pools where shared water cannot be denied. How much fishing they ruin by their lack of consideration for others is anybody's guess, but no fishing licence can enforce a compulsory code of good manners.

Regulations could doubtless be framed to prohibit some of the more objectionable practices which probably reflect the mental attitudes of a permissive society, but no regulations can serve much purpose unless they can be policed and enforced. The principle of open water is too great a privilege to be lightly abandoned. Nevertheless, fishermen who enjoy the generous freedom of Taupo should pause to reflect that their numbers are increasing every year, and that the surest way to destroy a privilege for the many is through the abuse of that privilege by a few.

I am getting no younger and I may be inclined to dwell too nostalgically on memories of the Golden Past. Yet I am forced to the conclusion that present pleasures are dimmed by a widespread deterioration in angling manners and that the future joys of new angling generations will have to be increasingly regulated and controlled.

I should hate to arrive at the Waitahanui or the Tongariro and be required to report at a fishing manager's office, there to be told, after inspection of my licence, that I could be allotted a certain beat on the river, or a certain position at the Rip, for a certain number of hours; to be time-clocked in and out of the water; to be registered, regimented and repressed.

It may never come to that. The way things are going at present, more and more of the fish-hungry folk may take to boats and lead-lines and the trolling of assorted hardware, leaving the rivers and other fly waters to those who are prepared to fish them according to generally accepted standards. But the rivers themselves and even the broad waters of the lake must still be preserved against the attentions of engineers, property developers and the purveyors of pollution.

Meanwhile the present remains pleasant enough in all conscience. It is good even to await the passing of summer in the knowledge that the autumn runs will soon be starting and that it will be possible to leave the crowded and talkative company of the Rip for the quiet pools and sparkling reaches of the river.

In my first season as a permanent Taupo resident, I did not take my first fresh-run fish in the river until May 14. In the following year it was on March 22, in 1972 on March 14, and in 1973 on March 28. Thus something of the old pattern remains. More and more fishermen may be competing annually for a fairly constant number of fish, but the harder the trout are to hook the happier is the sense of achievement.

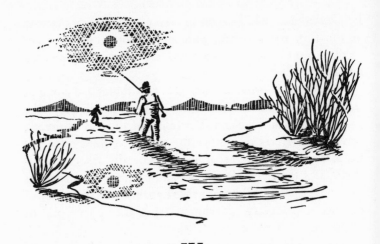

IV

VISITING FISHERMEN

In one of his gloomier moods, the sorely afflicted Job once expressed a desire that his adversary had written a book. I have always found the Scriptural passage rather obscure, but I have concluded that the victim of so many misfortunes had formed the opinion that if a man wrote a book he provided his adversaries with all the ammunition they needed for his destruction. Books, under such an interpretation, are self-revealing and therefore self-destructive.

Far be it from me to challenge the wisdom of the ancient Hebrews, but my experience has been precisely the opposite. My first book on Taupo fishing was published initially in 1955 and has since run through several editions and printings. Whether it was self-revealing or not, it has made for me a number of friends. It was at least partly responsible for gaining me membership of two rather celebrated angling clubs, one in London and the other in New York. In the years before my retirement I used to make fairly frequent journeys to and through both cities, and visits to my two clubs always proved happy occasions, with much good company and much good talk of fish and fishing.

Since my retirement, members of both clubs in welcome numbers have come to visit me. My home address is listed in the club membership booklets and it is not unusual for fellow members to write to me for information and advice if they are contemplating a trip to New Zealand and a few days at Taupo. It enlivens the passing year to have them call, sometimes to have them stay with us in our home, always to have their company on trout water and to do our best to find them fishing worthy of their visit.

For many years now I have been privileged to claim new friends from overseas through a shared enthusiasm for fishing. Since my second marriage in 1965, Cara, my wife, has accepted the position and, indeed, has rejoiced in it. She herself is a Taupo fisher of considerable experience and of genuine skill, and she was delighted when, a few months after our marriage, my closest American friends, Pete and Marg DuBois, came to spend a fishing holiday with us at Taupo. It was to be their third fishing pilgrimage to New Zealand, but Cara had not met them on either of their two previous visits. I knew that all four of us would have the time of our lives, especially if the fish co-operated.

We rented a motel unit at Waitahanui for the fortnight that Pete and Marg were to be with us, preferring its 'mod. cons.' to the rather Spartan accommodation provided by the Lodge cottages. The unit was small and we would have been tumbling over one another if the weather at any time had kept us for long periods indoors. But the March-April weather was as perfect as Taupo can provide and we had no occasion to use our cramped quarters for anything but eating and sleeping. The rest of the time we spent on the water. Even one night of heavy rain proved a blessing, as it brought a fresh and a good run of fish into the river.

We covered a lot of fishing territory—both Rip and

river at Waitahanui, a couple of excursions to the Tongariro, three days in a hired launch fishing the stream mouths of the Western Bays and a sortie to the upper waters of the Rangitaiki River in forestry country to the east of Taupo. Under widely varying conditions Pete and Marg, and indeed all four of us, managed to take all the fish that anyone but a glutton could reasonably desire. Pete fell in love with the splendid pools of the Tongariro and, even if he found the wading rather difficult, took his quota of the strong, fast-running Tongariro fish.

It was the year of the Muddler Minnow. A few months earlier, Marg had caught a record salmon in Norway on this strangely fashioned North American fly, and both she and Pete were convinced that it would interest Taupo trout. It not only interested them; it literally excited them. While Cara and I remained faithful to the traditional Taupo patterns, Pete and Marg took the bulk of their fish on the Muddler and became more than ever convinced of its deadliness in trout water.

The Muddler became involved in one incident that demonstrated the efficacy of an angling technique less widely known than I had believed to be the case. Some time previously I had been courteously taken to task in a letter from a female angler who reprimanded me for not having disclosed in my first Taupo book the Maori method for releasing a snagged fly. I had thought that the method was in fairly general use, but subsequent discussions with other fishermen have established that many of them had never heard of it.

One afternoon Pete and I were fishing a beat on the Waitahanui when I became firmly attached to a snag in the deep water of Poi Pool. There was only one thing for it— the Maori technique. I waded ashore, paying out line, deposited my rod on the bank, collected a few springy and leafy switches of manuka (a native shrub) and was just bending them into a wreath round my line when Pete joined me on the bank. He was curious to know what I was doing.

'Snagged,' I told him, 'so I'm sending down a wreath.'

I waded back into the river and let the current carry the wreath down my line. I had paid out ample line and, as the submerged wreath moved downstream from the snag, a gentle tugging indicated that the pull on the snagged fly was being exerted from the opposite direction. The tugging ceased, I reeled in and back came line, cast, fly and wreath, all intact.

'Well, I'm damned,' said Pete. 'If I hadn't seen it, I wouldn't have believed it. And I lost a perfectly good fly on a snag there only this morning.'

The next day Pete was fishing Poi Pool again and once more became firmly snagged. He was preparing to send down a wreath when Marg approached, mystified and curious.

'You watch,' said Pete. 'Here goes the message!'

The wreath floated down, performed its downstream tugging operation and Pete reeled back his line. Attached to the wreath were both the Muddler Minnow that had been snagged and the Muddler Minnow that he had lost the previous morning. There could be no doubting the evidence of the two indisputably American flies. Pete regarded the whole performance as something approaching necromancy.

I still do not believe that the wreath trick is of purely Maori origin. It must be fairly widely practised elsewhere, but it is strange how many fishermen have never heard of it. Manuka is ideal for the purpose and on most New Zealand trout waters it is generally readily available. But switches of willow or any other springy and leafy tree or shrub would serve just as well.

The trick does not always succeed, since flies can often

become inextricably attached to submerged snags. But it works more often than not and can frequently mean the recovery of a fly that you are reluctant to lose.

It certainly recovered the two Muddler Minnows, and they could well have been included in the complete stock of the fly that Pete and Marg insisted on leaving with us when their visit ended. In spite of their success with the pattern, I remained dubious about its use as a regular Taupo fly. In the following season my doubts disappeared.

Cara and I were spending my long leave in one of the Lodge cottages at Waitahanui. On the morning after our arrival I was in the water at five o'clock and succeeded in taking the only fish hooked during that particular session—not a very large fish, but still a satisfying breakfast. In the forenoon and again in the afternoon the fishing remained hard. By 5 p.m. my breakfast fish still represented the sum total of the day's yield from the Rip. Then Cara, who had spent the greater part of the day shopping and visiting in Taupo town, joined those of us who were still going through the motions of fishing. Within an hour she had landed four good fish—all on a Muddler Minnow.

That settled it. I also started to fish the fly, both at the Rip and in the river, and with a fair measure of success. The next thing was that I had to tie the fly for myself. I carried out an autopsy on one of Pete's specimens and attempted reconstruction with indifferent success. I then wrote to Pete asking him if he could persuade some expert to give me detailed instructions. In due course I received complete specifications, almost architectural in their precision, from Dan Bailey, a celebrated professional fly-tier in Wyoming. Ever since I have tied my own Muddlers and have supplied a fair stock of them for fellow fishermen. They still take Taupo trout.

The fly is a fantastic mixture of turkey feather, calf hair, deer hair and gold tinsel, with its most distinguishing feature a substantial head of closely clipped deer hair, clipped in the shape of a ruff or a toque after having been spun on to the naked shank of the hook right up to the eye. In a later chapter, for the benefit of those who may be interested, I shall describe the dressing in detail, including it among my selection of a dozen dependable Taupo flies.

The Muddler represents almost anything—a small fish, an underwater beetle or grub, possibly a nymph of some description. It can even be fished dry when I suppose the fish take it for some kind of sedge or moth. It doesn't much matter. The fly is not an exact representation; it is a caricature; and it probably appeals to an unsuspected sense of humour in the trout.

Pete and Marg showed us that the Muddler will take trout in Taupo waters. A year or so after they had proved the point—and after we had confirmed it—I was to fish with them on the Brodhead in Eastern Pennsylvania. If an American fly could deceive Rainbows at Taupo, why should not a Taupo fly succeed on American waters? Before leaving New Zealand, I tied a generous stock of Hamill's Killers on No. 8 hooks. It is an attractive fly with a hair tail, a body of red wool and at least three pairs of small partridge hackles dyed green and tied in along the side of the body with the body material. I fished for three days on the Brodhead and triumphantly took all my fish on the Hamill's Killer. Later I donated most of the stock to Pete and Marg, retaining a few to leave with friends at the Anglers' Club of New York. From this latter distribution, one fly subsequently encompassed the downfall of a lordly Atlantic salmon in Quebec.

On their three separate trips to New Zealand, Pete and Marg fished not only at Taupo but also on the Mataura River system in Southland, where there is excellent dry fly fishing for Brown trout. They made fishing friends there, as they made fishing friends in many parts of the world, and, after one of their trips, sent back to the Wyndham Anglers' Club, one of the most hospitable of all such bodies, a framed copy of one of the splendid fishing prints produced from time to time in limited editions by the Anglers' Club of New York. It was to serve as a trophy for annual competition.

Not long afterwards I was staying for a few days with Pete and Marg in their New York apartment on my way back from a business trip to London. A package was delivered to them in the mail. It bore New Zealand stamps and a Wyndham postmark, and it contained simply a tape recording. Pete promptly produced the necessary machine which appears to be standard equipment in most American households and proceeded to play back the tape.

It was a complete recording of all the speeches—and interjections—at the Wyndham Anglers' Club prize night, with special messages for Pete and Marg when it came to the handing over of their trophy. There we were, sitting in the heart of Manhattan, listening to robust New Zealand voices with their occasional undertones of Scottish dialect, all of it eloquent of the warm and abiding friendship that unites fishermen in different lands.

Marg is no longer with us. On our way to London in 1968, Cara and I spent some time with Pete and Marg in Florida, at their home in Plainfield, New Jersey, and on the trout waters of the Brodhead. Marg was not in the best of health then and a few weeks later, in London, we received news of her death. She was the youngest of the four of us. It did not seem right that her sunny days on trout streams should be thus abruptly ended. I think of her often—and always whenever I look in a flybox and see a Muddler Minnow.

Other visitors have been impressed, as Pete and Marg were impressed, by the essential friendliness of New Zealand fishing. One good American friend, Ed Landels, has been making a pilgrimage almost annually for the past twenty years from San Francisco to the Southland dry fly streams round Wyndham. He has fished with us at Taupo, too, but his chief joy is in pursuit of the Brown trout of the Mataura and the Mimihau. I once remarked on the wealth of fisherman's tales that he must have to tell back at the Bohemian Club in San Francisco.

'No, sir,' said Ed. 'I don't aim to risk having the whole of that Southland country invaded by Americans.'

That is the attitude of most visitors who fish with us at Taupo. Wisely, they do not confine themselves to one particular fishing district. They find different delights in different parts of the country. Ed Landels has lately taken to exploring some of the King Country rivers to the west of Taupo in company with Peter McIntyre who paints as well as fishes in that lovely territory. English friends, Pat and Felicity Wills and their son Christopher, whom we introduced to our favourite pools on the Waitahanui, went on to fish with equal delight in the South Island, but young Christopher, before his return to England, came back to spend a memorable week with us at Taupo and to take fish beyond all his expectations.

Inevitably many visitors from the Northern Hemisphere come our way with little real appreciation of the difference between the seasons. They arrive in January, let us say, knowing that it will be summer in our southern latitudes, but completely in the dark about the likely movement of fish at that time of the year. Probably the travel agents are chiefly to blame, but they sell travel, not fishing, and generally are ill-informed on what the travelling angler will experience at his destination. Yet whenever visitors arrive there is always some hope of finding fish for them.

A few weeks after we first became permanent Taupo residents, we were happy to entertain a party of four Canadians, husbands and wives, sent to us with letters of introduction by Rod Haig-Brown. Cara took the two wives shopping, while I drove Dick Wilson and Ted Price to the Waitahanui. We fished the Rip for a couple of hours without result or any real hope of result, since no fish were moving. I decided to show my new friends the river, not because I expected them to hook into fish there on a blazing afternoon in early February, but because they were so obviously river men and the pools of the Waitahanui can delight the eye even when they are empty of trout.

We proceeded to a stretch of river with which the Canadians became immediately enraptured. The bright, clear water sang cheerfully as it surged down the narrow reach into Poi Pool which Ted instantly claimed. I took Dick over the upstream bridge and down to the Lady's Pool, while I returned and went downstream for a little casting practice in the Fence Pool. All three of us were within shouting distance of one another, although we were all fishing separate pools of entirely different character.

The shouting distance soon proved itself, because there was a whoop of triumph from Dick, followed by a fairly considerable splashing. I forded the river and made my way up the right bank as rapidly as possible, arriving at the flat by the Lady's Pool in time to see Dick bring his fish to the bank and beach it. I handed him my priest and he ceremonially killed his first Taupo Rainbow.

It was a hen fish, bright silver and not more than a few hours out of the lake. On my spring balance it weighed precisely $4\frac{1}{2}$ lb. And the chances of getting a fresh-run fish in the river at that hour of the day and at that time of the year I reckoned at about a thousand to one.

On the following day, at my suggestion, our Canadian friends travelled by hired launch to the Western Bays of Taupo. Unfortunately I could not accompany them, but the Taupo commercial boatmen know the western stream mouths intimately and I was confident that our visitors would be well guided. All four of them hooked fish and Ted Price finished the day with five. Again they were happy beyond words, not only with the fishing but also with the wild beauty of the places where they fished.

Out of my study window as I write stands a young camellia tree, now fully six feet in height and ready in season to burst into crimson blossom. It was delivered to us a few hours after the Wilsons and the Prices left Taupo to continue their New Zealand journey—a gift for the embryo garden of our new home. Every winter since then the Firefall flowers have produced their blaze of colour. Although a New Zealand grown plant, it will always remain to us our Canadian tree.

Most of our visitors have fallen in love with the Waitahanui almost as much as I fell in love with the river in the years of my novitiate. Yet quite naturally they fall equally in love with the more imposing Tongariro. No two rivers, as tributaries to the one system, could be more different in character. The Waitahanui, winding its swift way to the lake over the last few miles of its course, possesses a rare quality of intimacy. Pools and reaches follow one another with little barren water in between them. The river calls forth a fairly high degree of angling skill, as the current is swift, the pools are not particularly large, and in many places it is impossible to follow a hooked fish downstream.

On the Tongariro the pools offer vast expanses of deep, strong water. In many of them it is possible to hook a fish near the head of the pool, have it tear a hundred yards of line and backing off the reel and still fight it and land it within the confines of the pool itself. Generally the river calls for deep and sure-footed wading. It surges and spills over a boulder bed. It is a river to be fished with a good deal of respect; over the years it has claimed more than a few lives.

Between its many 'five star' pools, the Tongariro interposes substantial stretches of white water—heavy rapids up which the trout have to force their way on their spawning runs. The alternating fierce rapids and majestic pools provide the river with the quality of its fishing, for the trout have to expend so much energy in climbing the rapids that they are forced to rest for recovery in the calmer pools.

When I take visitors to the Tongariro, or when I fish the river on solo expeditions, I generally concentrate on three pools which I have come to know reasonably well—the Major Jones Pool and the Island Pool, which are virtually adjoining, and the pool at the Red Hut bridge, a mile or so further upstream.

It was to the Major Jones Pool that I led Lee Richardson on his first New Zealand visit some years ago. Lee had written to me from California, saying that he and a friend, Si Arnold, were proposing to fish the Tongariro on a Taupo visit, and it so happened that they would arrive during my annual long leave at Waitahanui. By arrangement, they stopped at Waitahanui on their drive south from Auckland to Tokaanu, and over a generous spray of martinis at the Lodge we discussed plans for some joint fishing, while I also heard of their shipboard experiences on their voyage across the Pacific in the company of numerous personable young widows.

Two mornings later Lee and I crossed the suspension footbridge high above a brawling rapid and made our way downstream to the Major Jones Pool. Si, with another New Zealand companion, had gone off to fish the Island Pool. Lee and I had the water to ourselves and I instructed him on wading in from the right bank toward the tail of the rapid at the head of the pool and then, veering slightly back toward the right bank, fishing down the curving length of the pool.

The practice here is to cast a fly as close as possible to the left bank and to allow the line to swing and straighten through the deep water, fishing the fly as deep as possible.

After every cast, five paces downstream and cast again. The pool offers such an expanse of water that it takes the best part of two hours to fish it down thoroughly.

With the extremely light gear that most Americans seem to favour, Lee started off according to plan. I thought that his $4\frac{1}{2}$ oz rod was absurdly light for Tongariro Rainbows, but he had assured me that he had killed steelhead on it in Alaska and large Rainbows in South America. The rod, although light, was strong enough to carry a fairly heavy line and, while I waited for Lee to work his way some distance down from the tail of the rapid, I was able to admire the ease and proficiency of his casting. The way he worked the light rod made me feel almost apologetic about my own 12 ft Hardy 'Wood'.

After due delay and progress, I waded in behind Lee and started to move slowly downstream. I had just reached the tail of the rapid when a fish at the head of the pool took my fly and at the end of its first run broke water almost level with Lee. I moved back cautiously to the bank, coaxing the fish into shallower water, and Lee splashed ashore to watch the concluding stages of the battle and to inspect his first Taupo trout. It was not a big fish, only a shade over 3 lb, but in excellent condition. Lee was enthusiastic, but considered that he must have fished over the top of it.

We re-entered the water at our respective earlier positions and on the second or third cast I was into another fish. Again Lee came ashore to observe the landing and this time was frankly puzzled that he had managed to miss both fish. It was another 3-pounder. We were both fishing Hamill's Killers.

Back into the water, and half way down the pool I hooked and landed my third lively 3-pounder. This time Lee was frankly not amused. He was doing everything that he had been told to do; he was fishing deep; his fly was swimming perfectly; he was sure he was covering the fish.

So once again to the fray, and a few minutes later I saw Lee's rod tip come up, his rod bend into an arc and a splendid fish make a series of superb jumps from the heart of the pool. Lee lost no time in getting to the bank, and I followed him as quickly as I could. If that fish had shown any signs of breaking free, I was almost prepared to dive in after it. Lee fought the fish as if his own life were at stake. The light rod bent and quivered. The line glistened and hissed through the water as the trout made run after run, every now and again leaping clear and bright in the sunshine. It was a full quarter of an hour before the rod finally mastered the fish and brought it on its gleaming side to the boulders at the river's brim.

Lee killed the fish and gazed at it in speechless admiration. We weighed it—a full 6 lb. Then Lee turned and vanished up the bank toward the spot where we had left our lunch hamper and other surplus gear. Within a few minutes he was back again, festooned with cameras. There were four of them, two movie and two still, colour and black and white. I, who am no photographer, had to operate each instrument in turn while Lee posed and pranced on the bank, holding the fish aloft as if in adoration. When I had taken three fish from water that he had already covered, he confessed, he had almost given up hope. But now the sun was really shining.

On a second run down the pool after lunch, Lee took another fish and in the late afternoon we left the river in triumph. We collected Si Arnold and his companion and drove back to the hotel at Tokaanu. Lee wanted me to stay to dinner, but I had a thirty mile drive back to Waitahanui and my rather disreputable fishing clothes were hardly suitable for a hotel dining room. But at least I could stay for a few drinks and meet two or three of the shipboard widows who had taken in Taupo and Tokaanu as part of their New Zealand tour.

Fish Barrier: The falls on the Waihaha River and the pool above which trout cannot ascend.

Left **Hatful of Flies:** And the Waitahanui Rainbow that fell for one of them.

Right **Morning Catch:** One angler's bag from a morning on the Waitahanui.

Bush-Fringed Stream: An inviting bend on the upper Waitahanui River.

Strong Water: A Rainbow landed from the Major Jones Pool
on the Tongariro River.

Open Water: Fisherman's Luck on the lakeshore at Mission Point.

Picket Fence: Anticipation and action at the Waitahanui Rip.

Stormy Weather: A lakeshore fisherman braves the elements.

Rugged Country: A typical scene from the Western Bays of Lake Taupo.

We had a cheerful session and when I was leaving Lee walked out with me to my car.

'Say,' he asked, as I was ready to drive away, 'what did you think of the widows?'

I said I thought they were charming and very attractive women.

'Yes,' said Lee, 'they're swell girls. And not too demanding.'

Lee and I have had other fishing occasions since then, both in San Francisco and at Taupo, and we have discovered that we have mutual fishing friends in other parts of the world. Angling produces its own camaraderie.

Over the years I must have taken at least a round score of visiting anglers to fish the Major Jones Pool and to experience something more challenging than the Waitahanui waters. Nowadays I always tell them of one comparatively recent experience which materially altered my reading of the pool.

On the basis of my own fishing, I had come to believe that the trout in the pool always lay in the deep water and that they took on the swing of the fly, just as the line was beginning to straighten. Thus convinced, I paid little attention to the retrieve of line and fly, although on the Waitahanui it is during this operation that one hooks most of one's fish. On the Major Jones Pool, it seemed to me, the retrieve became merely an incidental function to shorten line for the next cast.

One autumn morning a few years ago I had the pool to myself and had fished it abortively for about the first quarter of its length. I was casually retrieving line when the fly stopped and I automatically paid out line to free the hook from its suspected hold on a submerged boulder. The next moment the 'boulder' leapt from the water in a flash of silver and hurtled down the pool with my fly and a yard or so of cast.

I had enough sense to realise that, if one fish was lying in the shallower water toward my own bank, others might also be there, and with a new cast and fly I resumed fishing a good deal more carefully when it came to the retrieve. I landed three fish from the pool that morning and lost another, and all of them took on the retrieve in water where I had never previously known trout to lie.

Since that day I have always fished out every cast with care and have advised my fishing companions to do likewise. Most fish still take in the deep water on the swing of the fly, but one nevertheless manages to pick up occasional fish on the retrieve. What happens? Do the fish, from time to time, take up station in shallower water, perhaps influenced by some change in the current or in the sunlight on the water? Or do they follow on the swing and then pursue the fly upstream on the retrieve until they finally decide to take it? One never knows with fish. The one safe course is to leave as little as possible to chance and to be prepared for a strike right up to the moment that you lift the fly from the water.

One of my good Maori friends, Tommy Marama, is probably still laughing at my discomfiture in such circumstances only the other day when we were fishing together at the Waitahanui Rip. The fish were few and far between and neither of us had anything to show for our persistent casting.

In fishing the Rip, I habitually retrieve a generous handful of line until the loop of the cast is only about three or four yards from the rod tip. I then bring the fly slowly to the surface before making a preliminary roll cast to lift the remaining length of line straight on top of the water preparatory to the two casts that enable me to shoot the full fishing length.

On this particular morning I had completed a retrieve and I went into my normal routine of the short roll cast.

As the fly left the water a fish erupted after it, almost, it seemed, trying to grab the vanishing lure in mid-air. Five yards away on my right Tommy roared with laughter. He was wearing polaroid glasses and he had seen the fish following my fly right up to the time that I rolled it clear of the water.

'If you'd left the fly there for another second,' said Tommy, 'the fish would have taken it.'

But we are neglecting our 'visiting firemen'. One of my frequent fishing companions in recent years is a young American, Bob Stinson. He is a fellow member of the Anglers' Club of New York and not long after my retirement he wrote to me saying that he hoped to spend a month fishing in New Zealand on his way to Australia where he proposed to establish himself in business in Melbourne.

Bob duly arrived in October, 1970. As I had written to warn him, October is not regarded as a good fishing month; it normally witnesses the downstream migration of spent fish from the spawning redds. However, the fish seemed to be running late that year, and we could always hope for the best.

On the first morning after Bob's arrival we proceeded to the Waitahanui. There was a brisk westerly after some days of rain and the river was running high and slightly discoloured. I put Bob into my favourite Flaxbush Pool with full instructions concerning the best casting positions, while I forded the river to fish the Kingfisher Pool about a hundred yards downstream. I had not been casting for more than about five minutes when I heard a tremendous shout and a terrific splashing. A hooked fish jumped clear of the water only a few yards behind me.

Bob crossed the river where he had seen me ford it earlier, still keeping a tight line on the fish. He squelched up and down the marshy flat on the right bank and with considerable skill kept the fish from running into and out of the Kingfisher Pool and round a left-hand bend which would have necessitated another and more awkward river crossing. Gradually he coaxed the tiring fish back and I re-entered the water to flick it up for him on to the marginal watercress. The priest and the spring balance performed their customary functions, and Bob gazed lovingly at a fresh-run jack fish of $5\frac{1}{2}$ lb—his first Taupo trout, hooked and landed within minutes of his arrival on Taupo water.

On that first trip Bob was with us off and on for about three weeks. The westerly continued to blow, making the Rip unfishable, but we took our share of fish from several of the Waitahanui pools, and on an expedition to the Tongariro Bob landed two fish from the Red Hut Pool inside a quarter of an hour. He disappeared for a time to fish elsewhere with Pat Burstall, but came back to us for a final day of Taupo fishing before flying off to Melbourne. The spring westerly had moderated and on the evening of that final day we were able for the first time to fish the Waitahanui Rip. And, as on the river, within minutes Bob landed his first Rip fish, this time a $6\frac{1}{2}$ lb Brown.

The next morning Bob had to leave after breakfast in his rental car on his way to Rotorua, Auckland and Melbourne. He would be back, he told us, most certainly he would be back.

A few days later we had a letter from him. After he left us, he wrote, he drove the short distance from our home to the main highway where unaccountably his car, instead of turning left to travel north, turned right and proceeded south until it stopped on the banks of the Waitahanui near the Flaxbush Pool. A quarter of an hour later Bob was back in his car and on his way north with a newly killed 6-pounder in the luggage boot.

'You bet I'll be back,' he concluded. And he has been back three or four times since then, fishing the Bay of Plenty and

East Coast rivers, the streams of Southland and the Southern Lakes and always, for at least part of the time, Taupo. He has trout water at his disposal in Australia, but Taupo draws him like a magnet. He fishes furiously and adventurously. On one trip he had a fellow American, Dick Rossbach, with him; and Dick had to come to us for a rest.

Then there was the American family—husband, wife and mother-in-law—whom Cara gathered under her wing one afternoon at the Taupo bus terminal. She had gone there to collect a parcel and discovered a lone woman looking rather lost amid an array of suitcases. Cara asked if she could be of any help and was told that daughter and son-in-law were across the road at the travel agents, trying to fix some over-night accommodation. They had come from Rotorua by bus, but her son-in-law, who was a mad keen fisherman, was determined to spend at least twenty-four hours at Taupo if only to look at the place. Then they would continue on their way south.

Cara took charge of them. She found them a motel, took them to a tackle shop where the son-in-law was able to hire waders and then put them in her car and drove them to our home. I was in my study writing and I was imme-diately called into action. Ed and Elaine Thomas, I soon discovered, were both ardent fisher folk but only Ed pro-posed to try the water that afternoon. It did not take long to fit him out with a spare rod and reel and an assortment of flies, and off we went to the Waitahanui where we fished until dusk for only one fish between the two of us. Unfortu-nately I caught the fish.

The next morning Elaine fished with Cara and Ed with me. Once again, only one fish, which Cara enticed out of the Lady's Pool. And then we had to drive our new friends back to town to catch their bus and resume their travels. But they had seen Taupo, seen trout water of surpassing loveliness and seen two fish landed. They were overjoyed.

That was in 1971. The following year I had a letter from Ed. He was due for vacation from his airline duties in Portland, Oregon, and he proposed to fly all the way across the Pacific for a week's Taupo fishing. He duly arrived and stayed with us for his eagerly awaited adventure. It was a shade too early in the season for fish to be running in the Waitahanui, although we both took an occasional fish at the Rip. Ed's was a river jack—a late or delayed spawner just back from the redds—and, as Ed described it, 'just about the homeliest fish I've ever seen.'

I counted on the Tongariro to make amends with its occasional February run of young fish. And so it happened. On two separate days on the Major Jones Pool, Ed hooked eight good fish. None of them was particularly large, but they fought splendidly. Ed was satisfied that the long flight across the Pacific and even the prospect of the weary return journey had proved supremely worthwhile. He, too, insisted that he would be back.

Some visitors have had less rewarding experiences. Our friends Johnny and Katy Hilson, from New York and Greenwich, Connecticut, spent some days on the Tongariro, fishing hard but abortively with the river level low and no fish moving. They spent a day with us on the Waitahanui, where Cara and I had been fishing with moderate success, but once again the fish were taking a day off.

We had fished the river during the day and the Rip for the sunset hour and, empty handed, had returned to our Lodge cottage for dinner. We had hardly finished a substantial meal when the front door opened and the occupant of a neighbouring cabin, Jack Luxford, walked in bearing a fish still dripping wet, a Brown jack of majestic proportions. He had just taken it off the beach near the Rip, and he had to show it to somebody. Actually, he wanted it weighed, and on my spring balance it registered 17 lb. Johnny and Katy forgot most of their past disappointments. With a flashlight colour camera they photographed the fish from every conceivable angle, surrounding it with a variety of household articles to give an indication of its size. Their own luck had been atrocious, but at least they had evidence that Taupo could produce monster trout.

With days like these, in the company of old and new friends, the Taupo year passes all too quickly. I would not pretend for a moment that all our time is devoted to the entertainment of visitors. They come and they go at odd intervals, but whether they come from England or Scotland, from the United States or Canada, or from nearby Australia, they are always welcome, for they are invariably fisher folk, and the next best thing to discovering new trout water for yourself is to show trout water that you know to others who are seeing it for the first time. Fishing friendships endure and our mail brings us constant reminders of so many people who came as strangers and who left as friends. Most of them, too, have memories to sustain them— memories of at least a few triumphant battles with splendid fish in wild waters and in a rugged landscape setting of surpassing beauty and delight.

A good half of true enjoyment lies in the pursuit of pleasures that can be happily shared.

V

CONSERVATION PIECE

Taupo fishing, the old hands say, is not what it used to be. Probably, like *Punch*, it never was. Yet, by world standards, most anglers would still class it as superlatively good. Many of us are concerned with trying to keep it that way. I have already postulated that sooner rather than later every true trout fisherman becomes at heart a conservationist. At that stage he must be prepared to do battle not only with the engineers, the property developers and the 'improvers' of the landscape, but also with the bureaucrats.

Even with the inestimable privilege of open water for the fisherman, the path for the conservationist in New Zealand remains anything but easy. Privately owned and even privately controlled trout waters may be virtually non-existent, but such a blessed state of affairs has not prevented the development of a managerial and administrative system that at times borders on the chaotic. It is here that the bureaucrats come into their own.

Trout were first introduced into New Zealand during the latter half of the nineteenth century by groups of private individuals who from time to time received statutory recognition and authority as acclimatisation societies. At first the district societies functioned more or less within the provincial system under which New Zealand for a time was governed. Parochial vestiges of provincialism remain as a part of New Zealand life, but whereas government became increasingly centralised, acclimatisation societies proliferated to such an extent that by 1968 there were twenty-three of them. Each society issues licences for its own district, polices its own rules and regulations and is governed by a council elected by licence holders. At least the fisherman (and the shooter, for the societies also control game) has a say in the management of his own affairs.

It is a say more apparent than real. Since 1908 control of all freshwater fisheries has been vested in the Marine Department, now dismembered with its controlling division incorporated in the Ministry of Agriculture and Fisheries, under which the acclimatisation societies continue to function with substantially reduced authority. To complicate matters, three special districts—Taupo, Rotorua and the Southern Lakes of the South Island—are under direct Government control and are administered not by the Marine Department or its successor but by the Internal Affairs Department, which has national responsibility for feathered game but not for freshwater fish.

A Commission of Inquiry in 1968 found that the stage had been reached 'where wildlife administration is shared by six Government departments and twenty-three acclimatisation societies, in casual and uneasy association.'

In spite of various proposals for administrative reform, fragmentation remains the order of the day. We are concerned here with its effects on freshwater fisheries in general and on the Taupo trout fishery in particular. One deplorable fact becomes obvious: Where divided control leads to inter-departmental jealousy and bickering, with fishermen themselves having little or no say on matters of policy, confusion is likely to reign supreme. The fisherman's delight in his own chosen recreation is at the mercy of opposing, disputatious and self-righteous experts, many of whom can never concede that in any circumstances they could ever be wrong.

Managerial control of salmon and trout fisheries reveals marked variations in different parts of the world. In the United Kingdom, for example, practically all the best fishing is privately owned. On North American waters, State and Federal policies are often in conflict, but private water has become largely an accepted fact. The famed salmon rivers of Norway have become centres of big business. Yet everywhere fishermen have had to band together to protect their own interests either from official interference or from official indifference. The war against maritime exploitation of the Atlantic salmon would never have been waged if fly fishermen had not seen fit to challenge the melancholy and mercenary Danes.

It follows almost naturally, therefore, that even in New Zealand, where open waters are the rule, fly fishermen from time to time should find themselves at loggerheads with bureaucracy. A classic instance occurred a few years ago when some of the backroom pundits of the then Marine Department became enamoured of the idea of introducing into New Zealand waters the North American large-mouthed bass.

The resultant controversy raged furiously and pro-tractedly. The proposed new adventure in acclimatisation was actively supported by a few acclimatisation societies in whose territories certain sand dune lakes and other waters had proved unsuitable for trout. The Marine Department experts were enchanted. A new species of game fish would provide them with additional administrative responsibility and authority. Parkinson's Law would almost certainly apply. The large-mouthed bass became a sort of symbol of official aggrandisement.

The other Government department most immediately concerned, the Internal Affairs Department, opposed the whole idea. It administered the three fishing districts—Taupo, Rotorua and Southern Lakes—that furnished, in terms of licence sales, about forty per cent of all the trout fishing in the country. The field officers of its Wildlife Division were on the best possible terms with the fishermen whose sport they controlled. Thus the department gained the immediate support of all the major acclimatisation societies in its refusal to countenance the entry of a species which could compete with fish laboriously introduced and triumphantly established over the preceding hundred years.

The vast majority of New Zealand fly fishermen rallied round the Internal Affairs Department. They were entitled to expect that the Marine Department, as the Government agency charged with safeguarding their interests, would heed their protests. But the Marine Department scientists, with detached obstinacy, insisted that there was nothing to fear from the large-mouthed bass and that a new sporting fish, in fact, would prove a decided acquisition.

Anglers gathered their evidence and thoroughly prepared their case. They were able to show that in the Pacific Coast states of Oregon and Washington, where large-mouthed bass had been introduced into Rainbow, steelhead and Pacific salmon waters, vast sums were being spent annually in efforts to eradicate the intruder. Although the spawning habits of the fish were different, large-mouthed bass competed with trout for the same sort of food. As the food resources of New Zealand rivers and lakes were not unlimited, the advent of a hungry newcomer would mean inevitably a reduction in the quantity of natural food available for wild trout which would suffer, with equal inevitability, a decline in size and condition. Nor could it be pretended that the large-mouthed bass could be contained in specific waters within prescribed territorial limits. Experience elsewhere proved that they would spread, either by natural means or by the careless hands of man.

Still the bass brigade insisted that they knew best. Politicians, however, occasionally count potential and problematical votes and then decide to have the last word. At one extremely acrimonious meeting called to discusss the bass project, the responsible Minister who was present listened thoughtfully to a brief statement by a visiting American marine biologist of world standing. When the meeting ended the Minister invited the American to his office for a private talk. Not long after that it was announced that the whole black bass nonsense was officially abandoned.

I subsequently met the distinguished American and asked him what arguments he had used to convince the Minister that his own departmental experts were wrong.

By accidents of geography, environment and human effort, the Minister had been told, New Zealand had achieved a stock of transplanted trout that had become world-famous. If the pioneering efforts had resulted in a breed of inferior or even average fish, there could have been no harm in an attempt to diversify the range of exotic freshwater fishes. But to introduce something that would compete with and probably detrimentally affect a trout stock of world repute would be sheer biological lunacy.

Simple reason prevailed. Those of us who had fought to preserve our unique trout fishery sat back and heaved a sigh of relief. The arch-priest of the large-mouthed bass, a man of unquestioned scientific attainments but with a somewhat lofty disregard for the angling opinions of laymen, resigned and left for foreign parts. We felt that we were free to concentrate on the unending battle with the engineers, the industrial planners, the property developers and others who, with or without official blessing, were constantly threatening the natural water resources that enabled us to conserve a national recreational asset.

We overlooked or underestimated the peculiar workings of what may best be described as the 'commissar mind'. Hardly had the large mouths of the bass addicts been politically closed when some aspiring merchants and traders conceived the idea that commercial trout farming could be developed in New Zealand as a potential export industry.

From the early days of their acclimatisation, trout in New Zealand have been literally a priceless commodity. By law they cannot be offered for sale. The rule was officially breached for a time some years ago when a netting programme was undertaken at Taupo for the specific purpose of bringing the exploding fish population of the lake into balance with the natural food supply. The netted trout were smoked and, by special dispensation of the law, made available for sale in the cities. The netting ceased when the trout taken showed a marked improvement in weight and condition and when it was considered that angling pressure had advanced sufficiently to control the stock. Thereafter the sale of trout was once again absolutely prohibited by law.

It astonishes many overseas visitors to New Zealand when they discover that at hotels and restaurants in districts famed for trout fishing trout do not appear on the menu. For a time it used to be permissible for hotels to serve trout provided that the fish had not been purchased. But the system was open to many abuses and was eventually banned, although hotels are still permitted to serve trout to guests who have caught their own fish and even—if the fisherman consents—to offer the delicacy to other guests as a gift from the successful angler.

Now and again some people complain about the restriction. They are chiefly hotel proprietors and restaurateurs who would like to be able to offer a luxury dish at a luxury price. In general, however, New Zealanders accept the situation that trout were introduced as a sporting fish and that, if anyone wants to eat trout, he has only to buy a licence and then catch the fish for himself. Anglers as a rule are not niggardly after good days on lake or river and gift trout are often consumed in the homes of people who would not know what to do with a fly rod if they were handed one.

To the aspiring merchants of farmed trout the restrictions represented an absolute affront. It was unthinkable to them that an edible commodity, readily produced in abundance under local conditions, should not possess a market value. Their interest was aroused during a period of intense political preoccupation with an expansion of export markets and the potential trout farmers swept into action with the cry of 'farmed trout for export'.

The fisheries folk of the Marine Department responded eagerly. Here was something new for officialdom to supervise and control. It mattered little that the record of the department in respect of maritime fisheries gave no cause for enthusiasm. The magic words 'export potential' sounded like a clarion call.

For a time trout fishermen could scarcely comprehend that the tradition of freedom from commercial exploitation was endangered, but it was not long before voices were raised in protest and made themselves heard. Solo voices soon became a chorus, and the Government of the day, itself wedded to export expansion, found it expedient to refer the whole question to successive Select Committees of Parliament.

The war was waged with an intensity somewhat at odds with the normally placid New Zealand character. Once they recognised the threat of commercial intrusion, trout fishermen in their various organised bodies took the firm stand that trout farming elsewhere in the world had proved to be a prolific source of fish diseases. With probably the healthiest stock of trout in the world, New Zealand could not afford to imperil a great recreational and substantial tourist asset.

If the politicians showed any signs of wavering, the Marine Department 'experts' were there to stiffen their resolution. They provided advisers for the Select Committees. They were in the privileged position of being able to oppose the evidence of witnesses against trout farming in the absence of the witnesses themselves. They were in open alliance with the commercial interests who sought a change in the law.

From the trout fisherman's point of view, one of the most disturbing things about the whole protracted argument was the manner in which officialdom changed its ground. Assurances would be given in an attempt to overcome specific objections, and within weeks or even days the assurances would be disregarded.

Initially the trout farming faction, commercial and official, pleaded that the farmed trout would be for export only and thus could pose no threat to a domestic sports fishery. Very soon the 'export only' plea was dropped and it was argued that all New Zealanders should have the right to buy the produce of their own country. It mattered nothing that the particular 'produce' had been privately introduced and originally privately developed for sporting purposes. What was that compared with the prospect of a quick profit?

In the early stages, too, the advocates of trout farming had argued that their farms would be stocked with fish raised from imported ova and would thus make no inroads on wild stocks or local hatchery resources. They were told that the risk of fish disease from imported ova could not be tolerated. Quietly they changed their ground. They insisted that there was no risk of disease from farmed trout, but they would furnish their farms from ova stripped from disease-free native stock.

The most solemn assurances were given that trout farms would not be allowed to interfere in any way with fishing as a sport. The next thing we knew was a declared intention to allow trout farms to operate fish-out ponds on which visitors, having paid the requisite fee, would be able to fish for virtually tame trout.

Again it was stated in the most categorical terms that no trout farms would be permitted in the Rotorua-Taupo conservancy. Yet, while Select Committee hearings were still proceeding, one potential trout farmer, with Marine Department support, sought water rights within the conservancy and in close proximity to prolific trout water.

By this time it should have become apparent to the politicians that the expert advice of their departmental officers was rejected by trout fishermen throughout the country. Yet a Bill to legalise freshwater fish farming, obviously departmentally inspired, was introduced and passed in the New Zealand Parliament even before the final report of the Select Committee was tabled. And that report ultimately, in its disregard for the weight of evidence, had to be read to be believed.

The battle continued. Petitions from all over the country were presented during the next session of Parliament, all seeking repeal of the obnoxious legislation. Whether by political accident or by official design, not one of those petitions received a formal hearing. Parliament adjourned, and a few weeks before a general election regulations governing the licensing and operation of trout farms were gazetted. They made some minor concessions to angling opinion by banning fish-out ponds and by prohibiting the establishment of trout farms in the Taupo district and other parts of the Rotorua conservancy.

Then a political judgment was delivered against official obduracy. The general election brought about a change in Government. The new party in power had promised that, if it attained office, it would countermand the trout farming decisions. And within days of its victory at the polls it proved itself as good as its word.

Such battles with an entrenched bureaucracy sound a note of warning for fishermen everywhere. Admittedly there are not many countries in which officialdom rides such a high horse as it does in New Zealand, but even in the British Isles and in the United States there have already been occasions when fishermen have had to organise some sort of united front against the pretensions of the remote controllers. Where such an individual and relatively unorganised sport as fishing is concerned, the New Zealand experience points its own moral.

Not all civil servants are necessarily tarred with the same brush. Although Taupo fishermen have little direct say in the management of their fishery, they nevertheless have an indirect say through the close and cordial relations that they maintain with the field staff of the Wildlife Service.

The staff that actually manages the fishery is all too small for the task in hand, but the men so employed are basically fishermen themselves, men of the outdoors who probably begrudge every hour that they must spend perforce at office desks. When the occasion arises they can speak and act courageously on behalf of fishermen. In one classic instance, senior Wildlife officers openly opposed the views of higher departmental authority in the heated dispute over trout farming.

Interference with the basic principles on which a fishery has developed is bad enough in all conscience. Equally serious is the widespread official tendency to jeopardise the long-term physical requirements of a fishery in the interests of short-term economic expediency.

One of the major Taupo tributaries, the Hinemaiai, rises in high bush country to the east of the lake. It flows over a meandering course for some miles before plunging over falls and rapids to run through a steep, narrow gorge until it reaches the pleasant lakeside settlement of Hatepe. Some years ago it was decided to dam the river above the falls to create a small hydroelectric power station. No immediate harm resulted, since trout on their spawning migrations from the lake had never been able to ascend the falls. Consequently the upper reaches of the river had always been barren of fish. The dam, in fact, enabled the Wildlife Division to conduct an interesting and successful experiment in the release of a stock of North American brook trout, Salvelinus fontinalis, in hitherto unproductive water. The fontinalis flourished. Access difficulties have prevented heavy fishing, but occasional anglers have managed to take brook trout weighing 6 lb or more.

Then it was decided to establish a second dam and power house a little further downstream. In the siting of the second dam, the local purveyors of electricity by-passed the Wildlife Division and sought permission from the Marine Department as the ultimate authority in control of fresh-water fisheries. And some itinerant experts from the Marine Department immediately demonstrated both their lack of local knowledge and their disregard for the first principles of fisheries management.

For more than half a century, trout, both Rainbows and Brown, had run up the Hinemaiai to spawn. The cascades and falls blocked their access to the virgin upstream waters, but on the left bank near the head of the gorge a gravel-bedded tributary flowed into the main stream of the Hinemaiai, providing the fish with ideal conditions for their redds.

The Marine Department experts promptly granted permission for the erection of the second dam downstream from the vital tributary. Its construction was rushed ahead before fishermen knew what was happening. No fish ladder or fish pass was incorporated in the design of the dam. During the first winter after the completion of the dam, the water below it, heavily silted and completely unsuitable for spawning, was literally black with fish denied the right to reproduce their kind.

A few years later Nature sought to make partial amends. A heavy flood swept away the silt below the second dam and deposited a layer of clean gravel over a substantial length of river bed. Some natural spawning water was thus provided, although not in full compensation for the lost breeding ground of the tributary stream. The future is problematical, largely because of heavy silting above the first or uppermost dam. Any removal of that silt by heavy flood could obliterate the newly formed spawning reach.

In other parts of the world, particularly in the United States, great care is taken in dam construction—largely on the insistence of anglers—to preserve access, both upstream and downstream, for migrating trout and salmon. The natural spawning waters of Taupo are admittedly generous but, because of man-made interference in other areas of the watershed, not so generous that any loss can be viewed with equanimity. We have already observed how angling pressure is increasing throughout the fishery, and it passes comprehension that on any tributary the nod should be given to any activity that could impede the free movement of the trout.

The biggest question mark of all hangs over the largest and most productive tributary of the whole Taupo system, The Tongariro River. With its flow from mountains and ranges snow-capped in winter, the Tongariro pours into Taupo about half the intake of the lake. For several years now it has been the scene of gigantic plumbing operations, with engineers blasting tunnels and canals to divert water not only from outside the Taupo catchment but also from the

Tongariro itself into a small lake, Roto Aira, high up on the slopes of Mt Tongariro, above Lake Taupo. Thence the water will pour down through a giant power station, but from the point of view of migratory spawning trout it will prove useless. No spawning water exists or can be created between the power station and the lakeshore. While the total volume of water entering the lake will be increased, the flow of the Tongariro itself will be reduced, with results that so far remain unpredictable.

All may not be lost. By some merciful dispensation of Providence, it was apparently decided quite early in the piece that, in matters of fishery protection, the electricity and works planners should consult not with the remote controllers in Wellington but with the district Wildlife officers who were actually responsible for the angling management of the river.

Engineers basically are not unreasonable folk. If difficulties or problems are pointed out to them before they are committed to a definite course of action, they will do their best to find solutions. Often they will accept the need as a challenge to their professional ingenuity. Short of abandoning the whole project and leaving the river in its natural state, the engineers have done their best to meet angling objections to many of their proposed operations and in the process have doubtless added substantially to the ultimate cost of their work. But that is as it should be. The cost of creating a new asset must perforce include the cost of protecting an asset that already exists.

A single instance demonstrates the value of on-the-spot knowledge and advice. As part of the whole power development, it was proposed to divert some of the upper flow of the Tongariro through a tunnel into Lake Roto Aira to augment the ultimate supply of water for the Tokaanu turbines. The site for the necessary dam and diversion works was provisionally selected upstream from the junction of the main river with its principal spawning tributary, the Whitikau, which enters the Tongariro on its right, or eastern, bank. In the course of their more detailed investigations, the engineers examined the whole area and discovered superior foundations downstream from the Whitikau junction.

Fortunately, at a joint planning session, the suggested change in site of the diversion was noted. It could have been the Hinemaiai all over again, only on an infinitely larger scale. The engineers soon learned that the Whitikau was vital to the whole of the Taupo fishery. They were given facts and figures that proved conclusively that at least forty per cent of all the trout in Taupo entered the Tongariro to spawn and of that vast seasonal migration a high proportion sought the gravel redds of the Whitikau. The downstream site was rejected; the proposed works were moved back above the vulnerable junction.

In another instance, the Wildlife officers had to convince the engineers that the actual tailrace from the power house to the lake could prove a threat to the fishery. The Tongariro enters the lake at a delta of several mouths where, on the completion of all the massive engineering works, the flow, while still considerable, will be reduced substantially below normal. Ultimately it will be much less in volume than the flow from the tailrace.

Unfortunately it is in the nature of migratory trout to seek the greatest flow of water when they are entering a given river system at the start of their spawning run. The flow from the tailrace will contain Tongariro water and its greater volume would persuade the majority of running fish to leave the lake at that point. The mouths of the delta, the gateway to ample spawning water of notable quality, would be deserted for the tailrace where, below the insurmountable barrier of the power house, no spawning water would be available.

Once again the engineers met the situation. They agreed to erect special screens across the tailrace at its point of entry to the lake—screens through which no trout could pass. The fish, it is then confidently expected, will follow their old homing instinct, cruise the short distance to the mouths of the delta and enter the relative sanctuary of the main river, even with its reduced flow.

How all these safeguards are going to work out in practice is anybody's guess. Seldom does man interfere with a natural waterway to its ultimate and lasting improvement. But the point is that efforts have been made to reduce interference to a minimum and to guard against forseeable dangers.

The Tongariro is a tremendous Rainbow river in its own right. To fish, with reasonable care, every pool and reach from the Whitikau junction to the Delta would take a matter of weeks. Considerable rapids and other unfishable water are interspersed between the various pools, and arduous distances have to be covered if the angler elects to proceed on foot. Many of the pools can hold comfortably three or four rods, provided that everyone observes the unwritten rules of the river and does not seek to monopolise, for hours on end, a particular lie. Over ten miles or so of river distance, on a reasonable day when the fish are running, the available water can easily accommodate, at any given hour, a hundred or more rods and barely notice them.

I cannot say whether any reliable rod census has ever been taken on the Tongariro, or on any other major Taupo tributary. With so much water and so many avenues of access it would be difficult to establish precise numbers—which, in any case, vary between week days and weekends and holidays. The Tongariro, like the lower reaches of the Waitahanui, is subject to an angling pressure that would scarcely be tolerated elsewhere. Yet, under fair average conditions, anyone fishing these waters has a fair chance of hooking and landing fish.

I happen to regard the river fishing as all-important; but a river like the Tongariro is important also to the trollers and other lake fishers who, season after season, are becoming increasingly more numerous. If the spawning potential of the Tongariro were ever lost, the trout population of Taupo could well be halved. The remaining fish might conceivably grow to great sizes, but the troller or the lakeside fly fisherman would have to labour long and hard for a much reduced bag.

Hence the need to protect not only the legendary Tongariro but also every single spawning tributary of the lake. Already in the north-western sector some streams are no longer performing their proper functions and the task of restoration may prove long and difficult.

In this particular area, over the last twenty or thirty years, land has been developed on a fairly extensive scale for farming. It is all pumice land which requires much mechanical effort for its initial development. Thereafter the pumice soil demands constant and heavy applications of artificial fertiliser, principally superphosphate, to promote and sustain the growth of pasture. The initial breaking-in process removes the natural soil-binding cover from the land. Erosion of one form or another quickly follows. Rain and wind sweep the light pumice into the tributary streams which quickly carry the spoil to the lake shore and deposit it in ever-expanding areas of shoaling silt. Spoil from hasty road construction adds to the burden. On top of that comes the run-off from chemically fertilised pastures, infiltrating into the shoaled lake areas, causing inevitable enrichment and promoting weed growth.

At least half a dozen streams which once served as natural hatcheries no longer hold trout.

The only immediate answer is to be found in the establishment of adequate riverside, streamside and lakeshore reserves, maintained in naturally protective vegetation to arrest and absorb run-off of all kinds. Such a programme has been undertaken in recent years and is making steady progress. The only trouble is that where land is in private ownership compensation for pastoral loss must be provided. It can be a costly business. Some areas as yet unaffected can be protected, but it may be years before the streams that are already heavily silted will again attract running trout.

Over a longer term, relief may come from a move away from pastoral farming and toward forestry. One thing about the pumice country of the Taupo basin is that it will grow exotic timber like a crop. To the north and east of the lake areas have long been developed as pine plantations to sustain a growing timber, pulp and paper industry. The trees mature in about half the time required in their native lands. Once the plantations are established they can be readily cropped. Given proper forestry management, there is virtually no run-off, no pollution, no enrichment of river and lake. And the whole enterprise can be just as profitable as pastoral farming.

The two chief agencies for land development in New Zealand are the Lands and Survey Department and the State Forest Service. Frequently in the past they did not attempt to conceal a conflict of interests. Nowadays a more co-operative spirit prevails. The Lands Department freely acknowledges that in certain areas afforestation may be preferable to pastoral farming. For its part, the State Forest Service, which once could hardly see the wood for its trees, is also taking a more enlightened approach. Whereas a few years ago most State forests were closely preserved areas, from which all intruders were banned, the idea of forest parks is now being widely accepted, and in certain areas anglers have access to excellent trout waters from which they were previously excluded.

As a result of these changing official attitudes, Taupo itself seems likely to benefit. Much of the land surrounding the lake is Maori land, under a tribal system of multiple ownership which hinders its development except in large blocks. It so happens that in the south-eastern sector of the Taupo basin there has long existed a considerable area of undeveloped Maori land—78,000 acres of it, covering fairly rough country. From time to time it was viewed as a possible area for farm development.

The Forest Service came forward with a different sort of proposition. It would lease the land from the Maori owners for seventy years, with payment of an agreed annual rental. It would turn the whole area of 78,000 acres into a new Lake Taupo Forest. And, as the timber matured, it would be milled on a profit-sharing basis with the Maori owners.

Here was something that appealed instantly to the Maori mind—an annual income from his land, the prospect of open air employment in forestry work for which he is naturally adapted, and after about twenty years the certainty of a substantial share in the profits of a sound commercial enterprise. Agreement was quickly reached and the new Lake Taupo Forest is now being speedily planted. That is not all. Other Maori landowners have been eager to accept similar arrangements for huge tracts of land to the west and south of the lake. The prospects are that, as the forests expand, they will gradually incorporate a good deal of rather marginal farm land.

The Forest Service has shown a commendable degree of imagination. It has undertaken to preserve existing stands of native bush and also to establish groves of decorative trees in appropriate areas to relieve the rather sombre monotony of the predominant Radiata pine. More important still will be the attention to be paid to the numerous streams that traverse the forest area. Protective cover is to be retained along the banks and on the forest roads all stream crossings will be by permanent bridges. The streams themselves offer very little fishable water, but they can and do serve as spawning sanctuaries, for which function they will be intelligently preserved.

The time may well come when a great part of the land surrounding Lake Taupo will be forest clad. The man-made plantations will lack the variety and charm of native bush, but they will serve the same purpose in protecting the watershed, preventing erosion, and sheltering the minor spawning streams. The total annual hatch of young fish from such streams aids materially in maintaining the optimum stock of the entire fishery.

For all the obduracy of the commissar type, an enlightened bureaucracy will generally listen to reason. The same generosity of mind does not necessarily extend to the private property developer who too often reveals himself as an arrant speculator in land values. As far as lakeside subdivisions are concerned, the wings of the property developers have been sensibly clipped. The declaration of shoreline reserves has proceeded to such an extent that relatively little land is available for residential purposes in close proximity to any of the more favoured angling settlements. Those who 'got in early' and established their permanent or holiday homes in strategic angling situations can count themselves lucky.

Our own particular neck of the woods provides a case in point. Not a single residential section extends right to the water's edge. A strip of land proclaimed as a public reserve intervenes. Yet over the past four years properties in the area commanding lake views have more than doubled in land value alone.

As a result, the property developers are now casting covetous eyes on the river valleys wherever they can find land that has not been legally excluded from housing development. Herein lies another threat, not only to any vulnerable river, but also to the entire Taupo fishery. Concentrated housing settlements close to a trout river can only mean, sooner rather than later, overcrowded waters, the exercise of squatters' rights in one form or another and, inevitably and most tragically, pollution. Not all New Zealanders are tidy people. Put a congregation of them in close proximity to a running river and they will quickly turn it into an open drain.

So the battle goes on. The remote fisheries commissar, the engineer, the pastoralist, the forester, the property developer—all require watching, however much they may insist on the purity of their own motives. The trouble is that vigilance must be exercised by individuals or groups of individuals—the fishermen who pay for their licences to fish for trout but who, apart from that, possess few, if any, statutory rights.

The Americans approach any such question in a practical and methodical fashion and very quickly convert it into a proposition in dollars and cents. I recently came across a report from the Federal Department of the Interior, analysing a survey of American wildlife developments based on census information. From it I learned that the number of American hunters had fallen in ten years by 301,000 to 14,336,000, whereas in the same period the number of fishermen had risen from 25 million to 33 million. Total fishing and hunting expenditure had risen from $4,046 million in 1965 to $6,826 million in 1970.

'Fishing and hunting,' states the American report, 'are still a big industry of significant importance economically— a multibillion dollar pastime for those who engage in these recreations and who appear willing to spend more to do so.'

I doubt whether we can summon up the statistical passion of the Americans, and I doubt even more whether it is possible to calculate the real pleasures of fishing in terms of dollars and cents, or pounds and pence. But, on the basis of the American exercise, it can be estimated from licence sales that some 40,000 anglers fish annually at Taupo, devoting on the average about twenty days a year to their fishing and spending on transport, accommodation and all incidentals at the rate of about $10 a day. On such figures, the Taupo fishery alone possesses an annual economic worth of at least $8 million. Capital investment, direct and indirect, is probably something in excess of $75 million.

Simple arithmetic converts a pleasant pastime into 'an industry of significant importance economically'. While I, for one, deplore the approach, it is possible that only by emphasising the economics of the case can fishermen, anywhere and everywhere, hope to preserve and protect their own heritage. Leisure has become not the privilege of the few but the right of the masses. And leisure, as Walton's friend, Sir Henry Wotton, remarked, is not something to be 'idly spent'. Politicians and civil servants and the noble army of planners may yet come to see that, by conserving, protecting and even extending angling waters, they will be providing 'an employment for idle time which is then not idly spent'. Therein lies the most advantageous use of leisure.

Yet Heaven forbid that our leisure should be directed, supervised and regimented by a corps of experts. They pursue their objectives, these experts, with considerable pertinacity. An Australian member of the tribe goes so far as to proclaim: 'The day of amateur direction of the fish and wildlife resource has passed. The professional is now not only available, but his services are essential. The management of fish and wildlife cannot be effectively performed (when it is subject to) the inability of the layman to fully assess management needs.'

If any such argument postulates the 'Big Brother' role for the professional, may all the saints among the Biblical fishermen preserve us. The services of the professional are essential, but, as in most fields of enterprise, so with fisheries: The professional works best under the sympathetic direction of the interested and intelligent layman. Too often the professional assesses management needs in terms of what is administratively convenient, whereas the interested layman is likely to be more concerned with what is objectively desirable.

If some of the professionals had had their way in New Zealand, we would have been fighting to stop the spread of large-mouthed bass and we would have been at the mercy of the trout farmers. Fishermen know the sort of fishing that they want, the sort of water in which they want to fish, the essential decencies of their own chosen recreation. The professional serves his best purpose when he employs his professional skills to meet their needs, not when he takes it upon himself to say that ' "Big Brother" knows best'.

VI

WILDLIFE INTERLUDE

In modern English usage, 'environment' and 'ecology' have virtually assumed the status of 'blessed words'. As such, they are often trumpeted by politicians and officials in the apparent hope that the mere utterance of the words can save the landscape from desecration.

'Ecology' has been defined as the branch of biology that deals with the relationship between organisms and the whole aggregate of surrounding things, conditions or influences. In striving to preserve the Taupo environment for the purposes of a great trout fishery, we must also have regard to the regional ecology, using the word in its widest sense.

The trout, both Rainbow and Brown, are immigrants and we tend to forget that their introduction into our waters produced certain ecological effects. A common belief that I once shared is that, apart from the eel and before the acclimatisation of trout, no freshwater fish above minnow size existed in our lakes and rivers.

In point of fact, Nature's law regarding the survival of the fittest probably applies to two quite respectable native fish that have largely, if not entirely, disappeared—the New Zealand grayling and the giant kokopu.

The New Zealand grayling is probably extinct. Up until the 1880s it was plentiful in most coastal rivers. The Maoris called it Upokororo. They fished for it with submerged traps and regarded it highly as a food fish, as did some of the early European settlers. From contemporary accounts, the grayling was an elegant, silvery fish, about 10 in. or 12 in. long in its adult form. At some stage in its life cycle it apparently ran to sea. Its disappearance coincided almost exactly with the widespread liberation of trout and the most generally accepted theory is that it could not compete with the newcomer for the available food supply in fresh water. As far as I have been able to discover, the grayling did not exist in Taupo.

There is a remote possibility that the grayling may survive in small colonies, isolated in some of the few remaining secluded areas which might constitute a suitable habitat. If some wandering fisherman could discover such a colony, it would prove a matter of considerable scientific interest, but the chances are that the grayling has succumbed as an ecological victim to the trout.

The giant kokopu still exists, although it is now uncommon. It is a member of the family Galaxias. It attains a length of 12 in. to 15 in., although one recorded specimen was 28 in. long and weighed 7 lb. It is found in some lakes, but it is chiefly a stream fish. It is a voracious feeder and in the days when it was more plentiful the Maoris used to angle for it with a short pole and line, baited with grubs—the nearest approach they ever made to any native form of fly fishing.

Quite recently a fellow angler, fishing in company with me at the Waitahanui Rip, mentioned that he had observed a peculiar fish disporting itself with a group of young Rainbow trout in a pool on the river about half a mile upstream from the lake. From its general appearance he was certain that it was neither a young Rainbow nor a young Brown. He estimated its length at about six to eight inches and was positive that it had a pronounced bull head. He could not say whether or not it had an adipose fin—present in trout but not present in any of the Galaxids—and from his angle of vision its markings were indistinct.

I thought—and said—that the fish was most probably a small edition of the giant kokopu. It could have been possibly an outsize koaro, the species of Galaxias formerly most common in Taupo waters, but his estimate of length made the latter identification seem doubtful.

Identification, in any case, would be rendered difficult by the several varieties of Galaxias present in New Zealand waters, with added confusion arising from Maori nomenclature. The most widely distributed of the species are probably Galaxias fasciatus, which the Maori called either para or kokopu, and Galaxias brevipennis, which the northern Maoris named tuwharu. Galaxias koaro, which alone has been allowed to retain its Maori name, used to be most abundant in Lake Roto Aira. For the sake of simplicity, koaro and kokopu can be taken as variants of one and the same fish.

Some years ago I saw a giant kokopu for myself. In a preserved state it was brought into my office in Auckland by a member of the staff of the Auckland War Memorial Museum, not for identification but simply as a curiosity in which I might be interested. The fish had been caught in one of the many creeks flowing into the upper reaches of the Waitemata Harbour, and the fisherman who caught it reckoned that it was a 'native trout'.

The fish was about 16 in. in length, reddish brown in colour, spotted and with a very broad head. It probably would have weighed about 2½ lb. So there it is. The giant kokopu still exists. I have heard of occasional specimens that have been taken accidentally by fishermen in various parts of the country on both dry and wet fly. But it is rare in waters where trout have become established. It seems to prefer stable streams in bush country, but it is no longer regarded either as a sporting fish or as a food fish. The immigrant trout, by reducing it to something of a rarity, have seen to that.

The koaro, on the other hand, after having been rendered almost extinct by the early Rainbows of Taupo, have gained a new lease of life, although they are no longer present in their earlier numbers. They are essentially a lake dwelling fish, although I have seen them some distance up tributary streams. They spawn on the lake shore, seem to enter the streams as youngsters and then return to the lake. In the adult stage they attain a length of about 5 in. and both as adults and young (or inanga) are taken by trout as food.

It was their availability as trout food that nearly rendered the koaro extinct. Before the trout came to Taupo, the only predators with which the koaro had to contend were birds and the Maori with his net. The little fish were not adapted to withstand the onslaughts of such a hungry feeder as the trout and, save in Roto Aira, the mountain lake high up above the southern shores of Taupo, the koaro had practically vanished until man transplanted to Taupo waters the smelt (family Retropinna) from Rotorua. Within a few years the smelt became firmly established, shoaled all over the lake and provided the trout with such an abundant food supply that the koaro were able to survive. Indeed, young koaro and young smelt often form mixed shoals, and the Maoris, against all the protests of higher authority, net them happily and indiscriminately for food.

Thus trout, if only through their inroads on the indigenous fishes, have already influenced the Taupo ecology.

They have become the dominant species of aquatic life, but for their maintenance in numbers and in quality they require specific conditions—pure water, clean streams, adequate spawning areas and a regular supply of food in both forage fish and insect life. We have already noted how a ban on the use of some agricultural pesticides has restored to the trout, at least temporarily, a useful food supply of the native green beetle. It remains a matter of concern how other forms of land development may affect the balance of Nature.

Bird life plays its part, and a not inconsiderable part, in controlling the stock of any given fishery. The breeding potential of trout under favourable conditions is so great that if natural predators did not levy a toll on young fish, over-stocking would inevitably occur.

The hungriest predator preying on young Taupo trout is probably the shag. Several varieties of shag frequent Taupo, but the most numerous—and the most gluttonous—is the large black shag. Some of the smaller native species, such as the white-throated shag, are protected birds. Irrespective of shape or size, shags are traditionally regarded by Taupo fishermen as a plague and a pestilence. The birds can be seen at the river mouths and on the river, diving assiduously in search of young trout. They can stay underwater for a considerable time and swim submerged for considerable distances. Often a shag will be seen to surface with a fair-sized fish struggling in its beak. It will slap the fish violently on the water until the victim is either stunned or dead, and will then go through the most amazing contortions in turning the fish so that it can be swallowed head first. More than once I have observed a shag that has proved a shade too greedy. It will get a trout of about 2 lb about half way down its gullet and will then find that it has bitten off more than it can swallow. The bird's retching efforts to disgorge the fish are quite sickening.

The shag does not confine its diet to trout. It also has a

taste for koura, the freshwater crayfish on which trout in the best condition always seem to feed. Thus the shag is not only a predator on young trout; it is also a competitor with trout for food.

Until a few years ago, fishermen and shooters in the Taupo district used to take part regularly in organised shag drives, aided and abetted by the Wildlife rangers. The birds nest in colonies. Nesting places would be discovered in advance and then assaulted by armed parties of irate marksmen. But the birds were cunning. They would disperse after the first few shots and the slaughter never seemed to be sufficient to prevent plenty of them from reappearing on their fishing forays.

The trout fisherman loathes the shag for other reasons, too. It has been established that the bird is the initial host for a parasite that ultimately attacks trout with a worm infection. The eggs of the parasite ripen in the shag and are excreted in the bird's droppings which are revoltingly consumed by bullies, a small lake dwelling fish. The trout eat the bullies and the cycle is completed by the growth of the worm inside the trout. Any fish so infected is not a pleasant sight when it is opened for cleaning.

Nowadays the periodical shag drives are discouraged by higher authority under the influence of officials who have become increasingly bird-minded in the interests of the various protected species. The Wildlife authorities have conducted a fairly extensive research programme on shags and have convinced themselves, if not the fisherman, that the bird is a much maligned creature. They insist that shag depredations on the trout population are minimal and that, in fact, the toll of young trout by shags simply serves to keep the trout stock in balance with the food supply available for both fish and bird. Likewise, the researchers do not regard the parasite worm infestation as being at all serious.

So the black shag and its assorted relatives continue to

feed on Taupo trout and to be reviled by Taupo fishermen with varying degrees of profanity. The trouble is that the shag is such an exhibitionist as a predator that it probably distracts attention from the fish-consuming propensities of other wildfowl.

I am no lover of shags. They are ugly, ravenous birds. But I would hate to see any onslaught made on some of the other forms of bird life to which the Taupo fisherman has become accustomed. Matuku (the native bittern), the blue heron, pukeko (the native swamphen), kotare (the king-fisher)—all are creatures of the Taupo countryside and all except the pukeko are fish eaters. Yet even among fishermen they inspire a measure of affection.

The matuku, indeed, was once a prized trophy for fishermen—prized because of its plumage from which the most effective of all Taupo trout flies used to be tied. The feathers are barred, soft and long-fibred and, tied in the semi-streamer style common in New Zealand, with a pair of matched feathers forming both wing and tail, they made an amazing underwater representation of either the koaro or the bully. The native bittern has been on the protected list for years, but that did not deter the fisherman who saw a chance of obtaining a matuku skin for the production of flies innumerable.

The bird is not an easy target for the shooter. It is ex-tremely timid and it has developed concealment to a high art. Only when one was observed in flight was it likely to fall victim to the man with a shotgun or a pea-rifle. Still, the feathered skins were so highly valued by fly dressers that ultimately the Wildlife folk, to accord the bird its full pro-tected status, declared illegal any fly of any description tied with the feathers of a bittern, native or imported. It was a wise precaution, for the matuku, which once looked like becoming extinct, has taken on a new lease of life.

Bitterns today are quite common in the Taupo countryside, much more common than the average fisherman realises. They remain extremely shy and they have not lost their gift for concealment. A fisherman unfamiliar with the habits of the bird could pass within a few yards of a nesting matuku and not be aware of its existence.

Near the banks of the Waitahanui there are several swampy areas, heavily overgrown with raupo rushes, which form ideal matuku sanctuaries. Whenever I am passing one of these swampy areas, I keep my eyes peeled for the sight of a bittern, generally standing perfectly motionless, with neck and beak upraised, barely distinguishable from the surrounding vegetation. On the lakeshore the matuku generally frequents shallow backwaters where it fishes industriously for frogs, carp and other small fish. It may be detected more easily in such surroundings, but it seems always to fish near cover of some description, into which, at the slightest alarm, it can disappear like a feathered ghost.

From the river bank the matuku certainly fishes for young trout, fry or even fingerlings. I was approaching the School-master Pool on the lower Waitahanui one day when I observed a bittern carefully poised in the shallows on the opposite bank. I spotted the bird before it saw me and I quietly sat down behind a manuka bush to observe its activities.

The matuku was as patient as any fisherman could ever hope to be. It did not wade about in search of food. Apparently it had positioned itself where some swirl in the current, sooner or later, would bring food within reach. I watched for about ten minutes and in that time the bird made six strikes into the water with its amazingly efficient beak. With each strike it secured a small fish. And then I incautiously decided to light a cigarette. Masked though I was by the manuka, I must still have disclosed my presence to the watchful bird. When I looked again the matuku had disappeared. It had not flown away. If it had, I would have heard it, for the matuku makes a considerable commotion until it is fully air-borne. This one had simply vanished into the riverside scrub.

I inspected the pool and found, as I suspected, that it harboured a fairly large congregation of trout fry. The little fish were feeding avidly on some microscopic form of insect life in the shallows, and the matuku, merely by waiting for the little fish to come to him, had taken its share of them.

The blue heron is a fisherman of equal persistence and patience. Strictly it should be referred to as the white-faced heron. It is a fairly common bird in the Taupo district, much more common than the matuku and not nearly as timid. I am not sufficient of an ornithologist to know the life span or nesting habits of the bird, but I have convinced myself over the last few years that I have formed a personal attachment for a particular pair of blue herons.

I first noticed the birds in the early spring of the first year of our permanent Taupo residence, and every succeeding spring I have waited for their first appearance in their lazy, angular flight near the Fence Pool. They nest, this one pair (or it may be successive pairs) in a tall bluegum tree, and every season I give them a passing wave of greeting when first I see them.

Whenever the birds are in residence, I watch them stalking quietly in the river shallows or fishing with equal precision and skill off the beach near the Rip. The heron is not quite as stationary a fisherman as the matuku. He will wade in search of his fish, but he wades with infinite care. He will stand motionless for minutes on end and then will quietly withdraw one foot from the water, thrust it slowly forward in almost a mechanical sort of rhythm and stealthily proceed to the next selected fishing ground. There is never a ripple on the water until suddenly a beak flashes down like a spear, and never once have I seen a heron's beak reappear without a fish.

In the early period of their nesting the birds generally

fish solo. Possibly it is the male that fishes while the female guards and hatches her eggs. As spring advances into summer—and as the chicks, I suppose, develop considerable appetites—the parent birds often fish in company and seem to maintain a precise patrol over any given stretch of water. The heron's eye for a fish must be as keen as its patience is monumental.

The rarer and more lordly kotuku, the white heron, is seldom seen at Taupo, but it is every bit as good a fisherman as its steel-blue cousin. When the kotuku leaves its one known nesting place in the remote Fiordland of the South Island it appears in the oddest places and, like the blue heron, generally takes up residence in its selected fishing area for quite some time.

Several years ago a white heron installed itself in solitary splendour near the Roto Ngaio lagoon, on the southern shores of the Waitahanui bay. The local Maoris were profoundly impressed. They made whole family pilgrimages to observe the lone kotuku and discussed its presence gravely among themselves, with much earnest speculation about what good fortune its visit portended.

I was sufficiently interested to drive along the rough and ready track to Roto Ngaio in an effort to see the bird for myself, and after about an hour's patient watching I succeeded. The kotuku appeared on the shore of the lagoon, wading delicately in search of small fish. It was the first white heron I had ever seen, but several years later, in Auckland, I observed others wading off the mudflats alongside a motorway on the outskirts of the city.

I did not tell my Maori friends at Taupo about this second sighting. They insist that you see only one kotuku in a lifetime. That means good fortune, but if you see more than one something terrible is likely to happen.

Whether I shall ever see another white heron at Taupo I do not know, but the blue heron is an agreeable fishing companion whenever it appears. Yet the fact remains that, as far as trout are concerned, both the heron and the bittern are predators. To what extent they contribute to the high rate of mortality among trout fry, nobody seems to know, but the experts will argue that their depredations are essential to the natural scheme of things.

The same argument applies to the less spectacular foraging by wild duck of the several different species that frequent the Taupo fishery. The native grey duck is the most numerous, but the black teal, the grey teal, the large and attractive Paradise duck, the shoveler, the imported mallard and the little dabchick are all fairly common. Most of them seem to divide their time between lakeshore and river valley, but it is probably only on the upper reaches of the rivers that they operate to any extent as predators. If female trout are unwise enough to carry out their spawning excavations in fairly shallow water, wild duck will scoop and shovel in the gravel redds to feed on newly deposited trout eggs.

Their depredations are probably insignificant, and in any case wild duck are such attractive creatures that Taupo waters would be the poorer for their absence. The native grey duck is the most popular game bird and for eleven months of the year it is almost tame. It will take up residence on the edge of some convenient backwater of a well-fished pool and will observe the antics of any casting fisherman with mild curiosity.

Not long after we were married, Cara and I spent a long holiday in one of the Lodge cottages at Waitahanui. The cottage backed on to a bend of the little Mangamutu stream and hardly had we taken up residence when a matronly grey duck swam sedately down the creek, guiding and guarding her nine attendant ducklings. They congregated in shallows near the back door and quietly awaited food. We fed them regularly for three weeks and we could almost have set our watches by their daily breakfast appearance. The ducklings became so tame that they would leave the water and parade right up to the back porch in eager anticipation of food scraps.

Only once was there any disturbance. The family party were just assembling at breakfast time when down the stream came another duck with a single duckling. The matriarch of our regular callers took instant and indignant affront. She advanced belligerently on the intruders. We heard and witnessed a tremendous quacking and splashing before the intruders moved off, leaving the original family in undisputed possession of their free-loading.

The grey duck is like that for eleven months of the year —quite friendly, mildly inquisitive, attractive to watch whether on the water or in swift and lovely flight. But as the first Saturday in May approaches the entire duck population seems to be guided by some wild protective sense. By that time the ducklings of the earlier spring and summer months are well-grown young birds, fully able to fend for themselves. With the first fusillade of shots on a misty May morning, the ducks seek sanctuary, either in protected waters or else high up the river valleys where they probably make their first exploratory onslaughts on the redds of the early spawning trout.

The Paradise duck is much more a bird of the back country and much more suspicious of human presence than the native grey. In all my years on trout rivers and on the lakeshore, I have only once seen Paradise duck other than on the wing; and then, invariably, you will sight not one bird, but a pair. The birds are reputed to be exceptionally long-lived, and they mate for life. They are large birds, more of the size of geese than duck, and they are attractively plumaged. With their preference for high country river valleys, they probably outdo the native grey in any sporadic invasions of trout spawning redds.

The black feathers flecked with white from the Paradise duck make an excellent trout fly in substitution for the grey or bronze of the mallard. I once tied a variant of the standard Blue Charm, using Paradise instead of mallard for the wing. I had sufficient success with it over a season to become convinced that the dressers of Scottish salmon flies would give small fortunes for Paradise skins.

I have never shot game in my life, although I have never failed to do justice to a good duck dinner when it comes my way. I suppose my very amateur interest in the birds springs naturally from their presence on trout waters. There I find them a natural adornment to the scene, whatever part they may play in preserving the ecological balance.

On two occasions at Taupo I have observed congregations of waterfowl that had to be seen to be believed. The first occasion was not long after the establishment of brook trout above the newly created upper dam on the Hinemaiai. I went there to spend a day with a party of Wildlife rangers who were netting a couple of tributary streams to mark the first season's crop of young fish.

Pat Burstall met me at the dam on a misty autumnal morning and rowed me up to the head of the lake in an ancient, flat-bottomed punt. The man-made lake was shallow but quite extensive in area, with clumps of manuka protruding from occasional underwater humps and hillocks. The route up the lake had to be flagged with strips of cloth hanging from the spectral manuka.

Then, as we proceeded slowly through the mist, the wildlife of the lake started to take shape. Swans with their cygnets sailed eerily into view. Wild geese cackled angrily at our presence. Duck of several different species abounded, either in pairs or in small groups. The little dabchicks dived industriously. It was impossible to estimate the total population of birds, so widely were they dispersed.

A few years later Doggy White and I revisited the lake,

hoping to borrow the caretaker's boat and to fish for brook trout. As luck would have it, the caretaker was absent and the oars were missing from his beached boat. But our visit was not wasted. Over the intervening years, the lake, by silting from upstream, had contracted substantially in area, but it still represented a fair expanse of water which, to our amazement, was almost covered with waterfowl. Some of the swans—or their descendants—were still there, but the wild duck must have been present in their thousands—greys and Paradise and teal and mallard.

Doggy, who knows much more about wild duck than I will ever learn, reckoned that just about every New Zealand species was present. When I ventured the opinion that a small and exclusive group in a little sheltered bay could even be the rare New Zealand blue duck, Doggy was inclined to agree with me. We could not get near enough to make identification possible. Yet the whole spectacle was one that I shall never forget. I wondered what raptures a man like Peter Scott would have experienced if he could have observed it.

My most recent visit to the upper Hinemaiai was only a year or so ago. The silting had progressed ruinously and the little lake was reduced virtually to the size of a large pond. Not a single specimen of waterfowl was in sight.

Perhaps the birds may return in season. Or perhaps they have cleaned out the lavish food supply that a newly created lake afforded. But silt is the menace, clogging the water and rendering it barren. The trouble is that what has happened on the Hinemaiai can happen and is happening elsewhere.

The significance of all this bird lore is that trout and waterfowl, as far as I can judge, seem to be able to exist together if not quite happily at least with a certain degree of mutual respect and tolerance. I shall continue to detest the black shag as a matter of principle or prejudice, but I am prepared to go along with the bird folk of the Wildlife

Service in their assertion that some degree of natural predation is necessary to keep everything in balance.

After all, the female Rainbow in spawning, so the experts tell us, deposits nine hundred eggs for every pound of her weight. The rate of fertilisation by the male fish, under what seems a rather hit-or-miss system of reproduction, is exceptionally high, as is the hatching rate from the redds under normal and natural conditions. Thus, if there were even a 50 per cent survival rate from fertilised and hatched ova, the progeny of three female and one male fish in a single spawning season could number upward of six thousand. If a 50 per cent survival rate continued from the alevin to the fingerling stage, that would still mean three thousand young fish resulting from the spawning raptures of four.

Such proliferation of breeding, when multiplied by the estimated number of spawning fish that enter every average Taupo tributary, would soon become completely unsupportable. Even in a lake of 240 square miles, with an average depth of 360 ft, there would soon be hardly fin room left for the fish, while the pressure on natural food resources would soon prove impossible to sustain. Nature would probably adjust the balance again by ensuring that every mature fish in the lake turned cannibal.

Fortunately no such considerations need apply. Nature sees to it that mortality in spawning is fairly high and that subsequent losses by flood, by other natural causes and by natural predation reduce the survival rate still further. All that remains is for the harvest of fish by anglers to be maintained at such a level that the residual stock of the fishery continues in balance with its food supply. The only fly in the ointment is that the angling harvest, if it becomes excessive, must be restricted, since it is much more readily controlled than natural loss or predation.

Quite apart from water fowl, the bird life of Taupo is

prolific. The native songsters, the tui and the bellbird, are seldom absent. The shining cuckoo returns every spring after its winter migration to the tropics. And above all others, the most friendly and most attractive of our small native birds, the fantail, is a creature of trout streams.

Only since I became a permanent resident of Taupo have I learned that piwakawaka, the fantail, at least in our part of the country, is predominantly a bird of winter. They flutter about most New Zealand bush country all the year round, but at Taupo in the winter they appear in flocks. In the colder months, whenever I take a rod for a walk on river or stream, I know for certain that fantails will keep me company. No matter how blustery the day, they will be darting and pirouetting over the surface of the water, at times almost skimming the current and at other times sweeping fantastically to the topmost branches of the riverside manuka.

They do not confine themselves in winter to the river valleys. Even in residential areas, so long as there is reasonable vegetation, fantails will bring life to the scene, performing their miracles of eccentric flight from dawn to dusk.

Certain types of foliage, I suppose, serve as hatching grounds for the minute insects on which the birds feed, and the cheerful little hunters pursue their prey with fantastic energy. They have little fear of human beings, and an open door or window will bring them inside the house on twittering and excited visits of inspection. They swoop inside the sitting room, perch on lamp brackets, spread and fold their lovely little fans and prepare to leave only when they have proved to their own satisfaction that the insect supply is inferior.

One such recent visitor alighted on the rabbit's ear aerial of our television set and seemed delighted at the way in which the perch would move under the insubstantial pressure of a fantail's weight. When the bird left, Cara, my wife, was convinced that it had adjusted the aerial to perfection and that reception had never been better.

Yet the flight of fantails above trout water is the most charming sight of all. The insects that the birds pursue seem to be in the main terrestrials, although the birds may well be competing with trout fry for a potential source of food. The young fish will consume any quantity of fly that falls on the water, which means only the proportion of the hatch that escapes the mercurial hunting of the fantail.

Watching the birds in flight, I often think that the spreading tails which so adorn them serve a variety of purposes. By the spread and positioning of the tail, the bird seems to make it act as a power brake, as a rudder, as an elevator or as a wing flap for whatever variation in flight it chooses to perform.

All is done with such economy of effort; all is done with a grace and artistry which few other creatures achieve in their pursuit of food.

Some time ago I watched on television a performance by a troupe of New Zealand dancers in Japan. They were rather ridiculously costumed to represent fantails and they capered and cavorted round an enclosed courtyard in a fashion that must have puzzled the watching Japanese.

Later, on a lovely stretch of trout water, I saw about twenty fantails in a live and authentic performance, and I thought how foolish and even presumptuous we mortals are to try to simulate the beauty in movement of creatures from an element other than our own.

The winter activity of fantails (if it is general and not just peculiar to the Taupo environment) probably results in some measure from their nesting habits. They are storing themselves with food for the breeding season. Fantails breed at least twice in a single season. The birds start nest building in September and their nests are most elaborately contrived structures, lined with moss, woven with strands of cotton or wool or dried rushes or any other suitable material that the bird has collected, and finished off with spider webs, the birds presumably having already consumed the spiders.

The female fantail generally hatches four eggs at a time, the first brood in late October and the second in December or January. It is probably a wise dispensation of Nature that a pair of fantails should thus quadruplicate themselves in a single nesting season, for the mortality of the chicks at the tooth and claw of predators must be fairly high.

So far I have never seen a trout rise to a fantail and, all things considered, I hope I never do. Yet one fisherman friend of mine swears that a 7 lb trout that he took from a pool on the Waitahanui contained, when he opened it for gutting, the clearly recognisable remains of a fantail. It is improbable, but by no means impossible, that the fish took the bird actually in flight. When fly of any description is present over a stream, fantails will almost sweep the water in their quest for food. Certainly they would come within the range of a large, fast-rising and hungry trout; but in the vast majority of cases I would back the fantail to perform some sort of evasive action that would turn a fighter pilot green with envy.

At any season of the year the fantail, when it appears, adorns a trout stream. It even makes a hard and fishless day in winter seem a day well spent.

Animal wildlife in the Taupo country has ceased in recent years to cause any serious problems. Indeed, as we have already noted, domesticated animals—the sheep and cattle on developed pastoral land—give the greatest cause for ecological concern. Virtually no mammals existed in New Zealand before the white man came and thus all animals present today are essentially strangers to the native scene.

Not so very long ago the Taupo back country used to be alive with deer. Stalkers could obtain good heads within a few miles of Taupo town. In autumn, during the roaring season, the stags could be heard bellowing amorously almost on the lake front. On my midnight drives from Auckland for long fishing weekends at Taupo, I normally expected to encounter half a dozen or more deer over the last twenty miles of the old pumice road leading to the lake. Gifts of venison from hunting friends often augmented holiday fare.

Nobody worried overmuch about the deer except the Forestry and Agriculture folk. They insisted that the animals were a threat to the forest cover, both native and exotic, and were indirectly a cause of much back country erosion. The Forestry people in particular launched their own deer culling campaign which, since the declaration of deer as a noxious animal, has developed into a campaign of extermination, aided and abetted by the activities of the commercial meat hunters.

For some years now, deer in the Taupo country, as elsewhere in New Zealand, have been hunted professionally by helicopter. The animals are spotted and shot from the air and the carcases air-lifted out to be butchered for export, so that venison from New Zealand appears not infrequently on restaurant tables in Europe and in the United States. Deerstalking for sport has become an arduous and problematical undertaking.

Just as the foresters and the meat hunters have slaughtered the deer, so too have the agricultural experts and the farmers dealt out death and destruction among the local population of rabbits and hares. These smaller creatures of the wild used to be present in large numbers over most of the Taupo country. A campaign of extermination has come very close to complete success, but it does not seem to have affected greatly the stoats and weasels that still pursue their stealthy ways in the bush, probably with some considerable toll on bird life.

Two introduced mammals remain to dominate animal wildlife—the wild pig and the opossum. The wild pig causes relatively little trouble and still affords some form of sport for the back country hunter. Nevertheless the wild tusker can prove a fairly fearsome sort of customer. There is a pool some distance up the Waitahanui known as the Pig Pool since the day when one of my fishing friends was challenged for its occupancy by a large and extremely belligerent wild boar. The pig crashed through the surrounding scrub and advanced so menacingly that Albert had to leave the shallows of the pool and wade out into the current as deep as his waders would permit. Angler and animal then viewed each other with mutual hostility until the pig finally departed.

Opossums are nocturnal creatures. They swarm all over the Taupo countryside, invade areas of human habitation, raid fruit trees in season with an avidity that would put small boys to shame and breed with such fecundity that the nightly mortality on the highways seems to make little impression on their numbers. The Taupo opossum probably ranks as the most careless of all pedestrians. On their nocturnal wanderings they cannot see a road without wanting to cross it. Blinded by the headlights of night traffic, they die on the roads literally in hundreds. In daylight hawks descend on the mangled carcases, but the trail of dead opossums is never entirely removed.

The animals are probably just as much a forest pest as the deer, and sooner rather than later the opossum, like the deer and the rabbit, is bound to be subjected to a campaign of extermination. Anyone who has had a holiday home invaded by one of these destructive creatures is not likely to complain.

Feathered, furred or finned, Taupo wildlife is predominantly alien. Fortunately many varieties of native birds have managed to survive. Even the occasional kiwi can be encountered in some areas of native bush, and the gorgeously plumaged native pigeon, once much prized by the Maori for food, has likewise benefited from its inclusion in the list of protected birds.

The fact remains, however, that the regional ecology has now developed round the immigrant trout. Not only the lake and the tributary rivers but also the entire surrounding countryside have to be studied with a view to preserving and even enhancing the optimum conditions for the maintenance of a great trout fishery. It remains to be seen how far human intervention can be curbed for the protection of a priceless asset.

I am now permanently and happily a Taupo man, living comfortably in the country that I have loved for years. The broad expanse of lake, the rivers, the hills, the bush and the scrub and the dusty pumice soil are part of my life. I know full well that others will love the land as I love it, that more and more people will be drawn to this enchanted territory. Taupo town, on the outskirts of which we have our home, was a mere hamlet when first I knew it. Today its permanent population of about 12,000 rises in holiday season to something more than 40,000. Many of those who come under the spell of Taupo will aspire to live at Taupo. The pressure of human population will inevitably increase and, as it increases, so will the demand grow for all those community services that mankind requires for comfort and convenience.

In a young country we can learn from the experiences of older lands how to avoid some of the environmental errors to which civilised man is prone. We must learn how to retain areas of wilderness as 'paradise enow'. Continued urban development can hardly be avoided, but surely it can be concentrated within specified and suitable areas and surely it can be sensibly controlled.

The materialists will want to do all sorts of outlandish things in the sacred name of progress. They would be happy to replace bush tracks with concrete paths and geranium borders, all neat and orderly and geometrical. They would fringe lakeshore and river bank with hotels and motels and neat bungalows and allow human habitation to sprawl intolerably.

With good fisheries management, the trout will still be there. More and more fishermen will fish for them and perforce will have to be content with smaller bags, with reduced limits and with restrictions in one form or another. But the rivers and the lake itself must remain inviolate to the extent that they have not been violated already. Those of us who love the Taupo country must always hope that those who follow us will still rejoice in the music of running water, will still smell the tangy scent of manuka, will still explore quiet and lovely places, will still fish in the company of the matuku and the blue heron.

VII

MAORI AFFAIRS

For a true estimation of Taupo, even a fisherman must learn to know, to understand and to appreciate its Maori people. They are the Ngati Tuwharetoa, a proud tribe of a proud race—proud of their storied past and both proud and jealous of the lands that remain in their ownership.

Most of the Maori elders from whom I learned much in the days of my Taupo novitiate are now dead. They were skilled fishermen, courteous and friendly companions on the water and, once their confidence had been gained, great tellers of tales from the past. I fish nowadays with their sons and grandsons, many of whom I have known since they were children. One whom I remember as a boy, fishing happily with an improvised manuka rod, is now the deputy mayor of Taupo and a leader of his people, respected by both Maori and European.

The Maoris of Taupo claim descent for their tribe in rank and prestige from Ngatoroirangi, the high priest of

148

Te Arawa canoe, one of the fleet that voyaged from the Society Islands in the fourteenth century. Another of high rank in the canoe was Tia. Ancient tribal chants keep alive the story of that famous voyage across the Pacific to the land that the Maoris called Aotearoa—the Land of the Long White Cloud. There Te Arawa was finally beached at Maketu, on the east coast of the North Island, and the eager settlers from tropical Polynesia began to seek new territories for themselves.

Tribes descended from earlier migrations already occupied various parts of the country. Relatively little is known of these early tribes because the newcomers from the Arawa, Tainui, Takitimu and other canoes of the fourteenth-century migration gradually assimilated them either by conquest or by alliance and intermarriage. All the canoes of the great fleet of which Te Arawa was one were manned by specially chosen crews of men and women prepared and equipped to establish themselves in a new land, and they possessed physical and other attributes that enabled them to prevail over the Moa Hunters of the earlier migrations.

The Taupo Maoris still preserve their ancient chants and traditional orations to recall how Ngatoroirangi and Tia, with their supporters, made their separate journeys inland from the sea coast in search of unoccupied lands. By different routes, both arrived at Taupo. Indeed, some of the more mythical tales give Ngatoroirangi credit for creating Taupo by hurling a totara tree like a spear from the summit of Tauhara mountain into the great expanse of open land that stretched before him. The branches of the tree pierced the earth and water welled up to form Taupo Moana, the Sea of Taupo, which the great tohunga, with magic strands from his korowai cloak, then populated with the native fish, the kokopu and the inanga.

By all accounts, Ngatoroirangi was a tremendous

traveller. He explored the whole shoreline of the lake and in the course of his journey even climbed the snowclad mountains at its southern extremity. There he found himself chilled to the bone on the unaccustomed snowfields. He cried aloud to his ancestral spirits and to his sisters (who were demi-goddesses in distant Hawaiki), beseeching them to send him fire. With the aid of the fire gods, Pupu and Te Hoata, they sent him fire beneath the sea and beneath the land. From White Island, off the coast, it travelled under Rotorua, Taupo and Tokaanu and, when he knew that it had reached the mountain, Ngatoroirangi threw down a sacred stone. A burning volcano immediately erupted. Warmed and revived, Ngatoroirangi cast into the burning crater the body of his slave whom he had killed as a sacrifice to his gods in support of his plea for fire. The volcano, intermittently active today, still bears the name of the slave, Ngauruhoe.

Tia's explorations were rather less spectacular, but at least he gave the lake and the surrounding territory the name that survives. On his travels round the lake he noticed a high, rocky cliff, remarkable in form and colouring. He announced that it resembled the taupo, or rain cloak, that he was wearing—a garment of closely woven material with an outer covering of flax leaves, coloured yellow and black. Under the cliff he erected a post of sacrifice, fastened his cloak on it and named the place Tauponui-a-Tia (the Great Rain Cloak of Tia). The very fine secondary school at Taupo bears that name today, and the Tuwharetoa people still claim that the great rain cloak of Tia protects all their lands.

On their separate expeditions, both Ngatoroirangi and Tia laid claim to Taupo lands on behalf of their people, but it was not until eight generations later that their descendants, by that time much more numerous, made a concerted move inland and, by one means or another, proceeded to dispossess the aboriginal tribes. Over the intervening years sporadic raids had been made to maintain the claims of Ngatoroirangi and Tia, but the forbears of the present Taupo people continued to live in the vicinity of Kawerau, in the Bay of Plenty. They attained great tribal influence under the leadership of their chief Tuwharetoa, eighth in line of descent from the high priest of Te Arawa canoe.

It was a time of great unrest among the tribes, presumably the result of population pressures which caused whole sections of the people to move away from the coastal plains in search of less crowded living space. Fierce battles were fought among the contending tribes. Tuwharetoa himself, although a renowned warrior, was essentially a man of peace and extended the influence of his people by the arts of diplomacy. But after his death his sons marched on Taupo and in a series of campaigns, preserved in almost Homeric legend, completely conquered the aboriginal tribes and established sovereignty over the whole region. It was not long after this time that their people took the name of their great chief Tuwharetoa as their tribal name.

For something like four hundred years Ngati Tuwharetoa have held their Taupo lands. They formed strong alliances with neighbouring tribes and themselves became powerful and respected throughout the North Island. Even in the early years of European settlement and colonial development during the nineteenth century, they remained relatively remote on their high inland plateau. More fertile and more accessible lands beckoned the early white settlers, and it was left to the exploring missionaries of the Christian churches to make the first European contacts with the tribe.

The first Church of England mission station in the Taupo area was established at Motutere, on the eastern shores of the lake, in 1843, but the real missionary endeavour under the Rev. Thomas Samuel Grace did not begin at Pukawa until 1855. The Roman Catholics became established in 1889, the

Presbyterians in 1893. The early missionaries lived and laboured in what to them was a wilderness, but they quickly made friends and converts.

Not so very long after the missionaries came the trout. Indeed, the pioneer Presbyterian missionary to the Taupo Maoris, the Rev. Henry Fletcher, was one of those who made the first recorded liberations of trout in the Taupo fishery. Even at that time, at the beginning of the twentieth century, Taupo was still remote and largely untouched by European settlement. The Tuwharetoa people preserved much of the Stone Age culture to which they perforce adhered long after the tribes of the coastal lands had learned and assimilated a good deal of Western ways and habits, both good and bad.

The early European penetration of the Taupo lands was chiefly by bushmen in their quest for native timbers. The Maori soon became a skilled bush worker in the European fashion, as he had always been in his true Polynesian tradition. Ancient Maori canoes, meeting houses and carvings still bear witness to the native aptitude in the working of timber. It was not surprising, therefore, that the Maori took to timber milling and later to forestry work as a natural extension of his tribal life.

So, too, when the trout became established in Taupo waters, the traditional skill of the Polynesian fisherman also reappeared. For centuries the ancestors of the Maori, in their tropical islands, had been predominantly fish eaters. After the great migration to New Zealand the tribes that established themselves in the coastal areas continued to harvest the sea.

The inland sea of Taupo offered no such store of food. The Ngati Tuwharetoa netted or trapped the small fish of the lake, the kokopu, koaro and inanga, and they had their own ingenious methods for capturing the koura, or fresh-water crayfish. The technique was and is to bait and weight large bundles of fern and manuka and to sink them in the lake over a rocky bottom. The contraption would be left buoyed overnight and next day would be hauled to the surface and the resultant catch of koura shaken into the bottom of the canoe.

Koura are a splendid trout food and nowadays at Taupo they can be taken legally for human consumption only by members of the Tuwharetoa tribe. Some commercially acquisitive Europeans have lately been toying with the idea of koura farming, but that, too, will be prohibitied in Taupo waters.

Even with the limited natural resources of Taupo, the Maori of Ngati Tuwharetoa remained traditionally a fisherman and when the trout first became established he quickly learned how to adapt his native skills to the peculiar Pakeha angling requirements of the European. From the outset, although few Europeans fished at Taupo in those days, the immigrant trout were classed as sporting fish, and rough and ready rules were laid down to govern legitimate methods for their capture.

For a start the Maoris did not bother overmuch about rules and regulations. If they wanted fish for food, any fishing method was as good as the next—the baited handline, the fish spear, the net of woven flax, the cunningly concealed fish trap. But the fame of the Taupo trout soon spread and by the early years of the present century the advance guard of visiting anglers was descending on the lake. They came armed chiefly with salmon gear—huge, double-handed rods and the gaudy flies that had been designed for Scottish lochs and rivers.

The Maori might have been puzzled initially, but even the savage who fishes for the pot probably has responded over long generations to the essential thrills of fishing—the careful pursuit, the cunning deception and the ultimate triumph over a creature from another element. The Taupo

Maori instinctively responded to the sporting challenge. Soon he was improvising his own casting rod and tackle, tying his own special patterns of trout fly and qualifying as the guide and instructor for the visiting angler.

Casting came easily to the Maori, who possesses a natural sense of rhythm. Watercraft was born and bred in him. Moreover, his tribe owned the lake and most of the surrounding countryside through which the tributary rivers flowed. In the early years of the Taupo fishery, the Tuwharetoa Maoris issued their own licences and, guided by Pakeha experience, insisted on the observance of fair and just rules in the fishing for trout.

For the Maoris themselves, if the need for food became urgent, the rules doubtless were often relaxed. We have already noted the tale of the record Taupo Rainbow, a fish of $37\frac{1}{2}$ lb taken from the Mangamutu stream which flows into the Waitahanui near its mouth. My old friend Awhi Northcroft was the authority on the subject.

'How was it taken, Awhi?' I once asked him. 'Fish spear or net?'

Awhi gave nothing away. 'Big fish,' he replied. 'We had to cut it in two to weigh it.'

After some years of authority, the Tuwharetoa people decided, with surprisingly little argument, to surrender their fishing rights. They were probably prompted in their decision by an earlier act of tribal generosity, for, as far back as 1887, they had given their sacred mountains—sacred since the days of Ngatoroirangi—to become a national park for use by both Maori and European.

The men chiefly responsible for arranging the deed of gift for the mountains were Lawrence Grace, son of the pioneer Anglican missionary, and Te Heuheu Horonuku, paramount chief of Ngati Tuwharetoa and Grace's father-in-law. Te Heuheu made one stipulation. His father, Te Heuheu Tukino, had been killed in a volcanic landslide that overwhelmed his village of Te Rapa in 1846. Not without inter-tribal dispute, the remains of the old chief, one of the most illustrious in the history of Tuwharetoa, had been interred in a cave on Tongariro mountain.

In announcing his deed of gift to the Government, Te Heuheu Horonuku wrote: 'My father, who was over-whelmed at Te Rapa, is laid on the mountain, and it is my wish that he be removed to some other place. He was, as you know, a chief of very high rank, and it is right that the Government should erect a tomb (urupa kohatu) for him, because both my people and I are unable to do so.'

The chief's wish was duly granted, although it was not until 1910 that his father's bones were removed from the cave on the slopes of Tongariro and laid to rest in a vault specially provided by the Government of the day. But the gift of the mountains established a precedent. The three peaks—Ruapehu, Ngauruhoe and Tongariro—make a superb backdrop beyond the southern extremity of Lake Taupo, and today they serve as a magnificent winter play-ground for thousands of New Zealanders.

Then came the hard decision to surrender the lake itself. There was probably some discreet pressure on the tribe to do so. In their mountain gift, the Tuwharetoa people had demonstrated their own traditional generosity, and their tribal elders were probably aware of the mounting difficulties in controlling a fishery which was becoming annually more popular.

Under an agreement formally concluded in July, 1926, Ngati Tuwharetoa ceded to the Crown the bed of Lake Taupo, the bed of the Waikato River from the Taupo outlet to the Huka Falls, and the beds of the main tributary rivers running into the lake, together with a chain right-of-way for public access round the lakeshore and on the river banks.

Financial considerations naturally entered into the arrangement. It was agreed that the Tuwharetoa people, in return for their surrender of the Taupo fishing rights, would receive an annual payment of £3,000 (now $6,000 in New Zealand currency), plus half of the annual fishing licence revenue in excess of $6,000. As licence sales now yield about $60,000 a year, the Tuwharetoa Trust Board, specially established under the 1924 agreement, receives annually something in excess of $30,000, the bulk of which it disburses in scholarships and educational grants for the benefit of the younger Maori people.

Members of the Tuwharetoa tribe also retain the exclusive right to take from the lake for their own consumption their traditional food supplies of native fish—the kokopu, the inanga and the koura. Some difficulties have arisen since the introduction of the Rotorua smelt to replace the depleted stocks of kokopu and inanga. The Maori maintains that the smelt is a native fish (although it was not native to Taupo), that it serves the same purpose as the inanga and that therefore he is entitled to net it for food.

It is a nice point on which even Maori opinion is divided. I have heard one old Maori argue that for years he had lived almost entirely on a diet of inanga; the smelt had been put into the lake to replace the inanga; they served the same purpose; and he would continue to catch, cook and eat them, no matter what the Pakeha ranger said.

Yet at the same tribal meeting another Maori elder took precisely the opposite view. The smelt, he said, had been put into the lake as food for the trout. Because the trout were in the lake, the Maori people received thousands of dollars every year from the Government. It was better to take the money and let the trout eat the smelt.

In all probability the argument will never be resolved. Fortunately the smelt is a prolific spawner, and the quantities taken, legally or illegally, for Maori culinary needs are unlikely to affect seriously the available food stocks for the trout.

Nothing can detract from the generosity with which the Maori people of Taupo have shared their birthright. The superb mountain playground, the great lake, the tributary rivers, much of the land in the Taupo basin acquired by the Crown since the early days of European settlement—all these constitute a national asset of incalculable worth. Some Europeans, I know, habitually upbraid the Maori for his failure to develop his remaining lands and for the high value that he places on them if someone seeks to acquire any portion of them. Remembering the musket and tomahawk land deals of the early days, the Maori can scarcely be blamed for driving a hard bargain.

Possibly some of the older Maori folk would not have viewed very kindly the gigantic plumbing operations now being undertaken on the slopes of their once sacred mountains, with river diversions and tunnels and dams and power houses altering the whole character of the landscape. To the old-time Maori, the lakes and tarns on the high Taupo plateau were 'the eyes of the land'. He would never have comprehended the astigmatism of electric power supply.

Some of the young folk nowadays gravitate from Taupo toward the cities in search of lucrative employment, but in the main the Tuwharetoa people stick fairly close to their tribal lands. The many fishing addicts among them seldom move far from the lake and its tributary rivers, and they are expert anglers in any company. They may not be quite as punctilious about angling ethics as were the members of an earlier generation first initiated into the mysteries of fly fishing. They have seen angling pressure at Taupo develop to the point where fish-hungry individuals interpret rules and regulations to their own dubious satisfaction and, in so doing, abuse the inestimable privilege of open water. And if the Maori cannot beat them he will join them, resorting to mass angling methods which the old-timers would never have countenanced.

Yet with it all the Maori remains essentially a cheerful fisherman. He likes company and, in spite of an initial shyness, will soon make friends even with strangers. Maori fishermen in a group will chatter endlessly and happily, yet let a fish strike and the Maori angler's reflexes seldom fail. Fishing at the Waitahanui Rip, many of them scorn the laborious process of wading ashore and playing the fish out from the beach. They will coax a fish into quiet water on either side of the current, do battle with it on a short line, lift it out by the gills, kill it, suspend it on a piece of cord attached to their waders and then carry on their loquacious fishing.

Gone are the days when their elders used to assist in policing fly water. Before his death my old friend, Harry Tahau, served for some years as an honorary ranger, appointed by warrant from the Government department that administers the Taupo fishery. He took his duties most seriously and when he was not fishing would patrol the water, carrying his warrant and other official documents in a small canvas haversack slung over one shoulder. It gave him almost a military appearance.

One day Harry apprehended a visiting angler industriously and illegally fishing fly water with a spoon. It was a blatant case. The man was fishing within sight of a notice board proclaiming that the river was reserved for artificial fly only. Harry issued the necessary offender's ticket and then announced that he would have to impound the fisherman's gear.

The offender protested almost tearfully. He didn't have a spare rod with him and his fishing time was limited. It was a fair cop and he would have to take the rap. Harry could keep the illegal spoon and produce it as evidence, but surely he wouldn't deny a fisherman his one available rod.

'I can't do anything about that,' Harry replied. 'You have to insult my superior officer in Taupo.'

Not long after that, Harry's 'superior officer', Don Main (the head ranger at Taupo in those days), caught one of Harry's sons fishing the Cliff Pool on the Waitahanui with a spoon. The boy was duly booked for the offence and his gear, too, was impounded. Unfortunately, he happened to be fishing with his father's rod.

A few weeks passed and then one day Harry encountered Don Main near the Waitahanui Rip.

'Don,' he said, 'when that boy of mine come up in Court?'

'He should have the summons by now,' Main replied. 'He's due at the sitting of the Court next week.'

'Ah, that's good,' said Harry. 'Then I get back my rod.'

Main told him not to count on that as a certainty. It all depended what view the magistrate took of the case.

Harry gazed at him in wide-eyed astonishment. 'Don,' he said in hollow tones, 'you don't mean to tell me that the magistrate would confisticate my rod?'

The under-educated Maori, of whom there are still many, does some strange things with the English tongue, yet when a Maori speaks English well he makes it the most musical of all languages. In pre-European times he had no written language, and when the early missionaries first undertook the task of putting to paper the phonetics of Maori speech, they discovered that twelve letters of our accustomed alphabet were entirely superfluous. It is remarkable that the Maori so quickly acquired a more complex form of speech. Today an educated Maori, or even one barely educated by our standards, speaks English that puts the slovenly speech of most white New Zealanders to shame.

The contrast becomes even more marked when on occasion the Maori thinks in Maori and speaks in English. Then you suddenly discover through a deep, resonant voice an amazing blend of poetic thought and musical speech. Among a people who originally had no written language, oratory was never the harlot of the arts.

Now and again a combination of Maori thought and Maori custom produces in English an expression quite startling in its impact. Once at the Waitahanui Rip, when I had waded ashore to sit down on the beach and change a fly, I was just about to light a cigarette when old Hoppy Wall limped along and sat down beside me. I offered him a cigarette which he accepted with thanks, and produced my lighter to light up for both of us.

'Let me see,' said Hoppy.

I handed over the lighter which Hoppy manipulated with obvious interest and pleasure.

'If you had two of those,' said Hoppy, as he handed back the lighter, 'I'd ask you for one.'

'I haven't got two with me, Hoppy,' I said. 'But the next time I come down from Auckland I'll bring you one.'

It was not cadging. Hoppy was acting according to his Maori lights. I was a visitor. I had something that he admired. Therefore he was perfectly entitled to ask for it.

On my next trip to Taupo I brought with me a spare lighter, charged it with petrol and at the first opportunity handed it to Hoppy. He was delighted. 'Better than box of match,' he said. But I rather doubt whether it ever remained in use after the initial fuel supply was exhausted.

One thing Hoppy taught me about fishing was clearly the fruit of his own lifetime of Taupo experience. We were fishing together at the Rip one morning when I was having the exasperating experience of failing to strike fish that merely plucked at the fly.

'You miss the strike?' said Hoppy. 'You change the fly. Same kind of fly, but smaller.'

Most of us, if we have hit on a fly that is attracting interest, will persist with it, despite the refusal of the fish to get themselves comprehensively hooked. A quick change to a smaller fly of the same pattern quite often brings results. Since that one piece of advice from Hoppy years ago, I stock my fly boxes with flies of my favourite patterns in three different sizes—Nos 4, 6 and 8—and if I miss fish I do not hesitate to change to a smaller fly.

Old Awhi Northcroft used to carry the tactical approach a shade further. Whenever he missed a fish on the strike—which was seldom—he would immediately change the fly. 'Not swim right,' he would say. 'Got to swim right to hook fish.' And Awhi was the master fisherman of them all.

The Maori seldom wastes his time in the water if the fishing is hard. He seems to know instinctively the climatic conditions that will bring the fish cruising in from the deeps of the lake to the river mouths; he seems to sense almost the day and the hour on which they will run into the rivers. And once the fish are in the rivers the Maori will spot them. It is almost as if he had some rare gift of underwater vision.

The Maori people do in fact have their own fishing calendar, but they are reluctant to discuss it even with close Pakeha friends. I have never plumbed the mysteries of the calendar, but I believe that it is closely related to the phases of the moon. Certain days round about full moon are apparently listed as poor fishing days, and on those particular days few Maoris bother to fish. But the Maori is no more a slave of custom than is the European angler, particularly the North American angler, who reposes implicit faith in the solunar tables and who arranges all his fishing excursions in accordance with some astronomical formula.

Neither Maori tradition nor esoteric solunar calculations can compare with the fishing gauge that an old Tongariro angler used to study for his own guidance. In the sitting room of his home at Turangi, close to the river, he had installed a substantial wall aquarium with a plate glass front. It was amply stocked with goldfish and other ornamental fish. The owner habitually rose early in the morning and would then walk into his sitting room and would study the aquarium. If its occupants were disporting themselves in lively fashion, he would get into clothes and waders, take his rod from the rack and proceed to one or other of the adjacent pools in confident quest of trout. If, on the other hand, the goldfish were lying comatose at the bottom of the tank, he would go back to bed.

I doubt whether the Maori could ever aspire to such refinements. During the first spell of unproductive fishing, he would probably kill and eat the goldfish from the tank.

Friendship with the Maori is a privilege not to be regarded lightly. They are a proud people, with their own natural dignity, their own innate courtesy, their own strong sense of custom and tradition. Sometimes it happens that a European, quite unconsciously, may befriend a Maori family in some fashion that particularly appeals to the Maori sense of family loyalty. To the European, the act may mean little or nothing, but the Maori family will never forget it. They are his friends for life and on their part it is a friendship in which no barriers exist. I know, because I myself have been fortunate enough to experience the enduring quality of Maori gratitude for a simple deed.

He is a miserable sort of creature who is not prepared to make friends with fellow fishermen on trout water. When we fish at Taupo, we fish waters which the Tuwharetoa people once owned. We invade their tribal lands. Unwittingly at times we may offend against their tribal customs. Surely it is not too much to ask that when we fish together we should offer them the courtesy and friendship which they extend so generously to all who gain their confidence and trust.

VIII

TACKLE AND TECHNIQUES

A fly rod, expertly fashioned from split cane, is a work of art and merits the respect that should always be accorded to any product of fine craftsmanship. Such rods may soon become collectors' pieces, if they have not achieved that status already. Fibreglass is rapidly replacing split cane in fly rod construction, and fibreglass lends itself more readily to precision engineering and the mechanical processes of mass production.

Nowadays I keep my three most prized rods permanently assembled, reeled and lined and ready for selection in accordance with prevailing conditions of wind and water. They are a Hardy 'A.H.E. Wood No. 3', 12 ft in length and weighing 13½ oz; a Hardy 'Viscount Grey', 10 ft 6 in. and 8½ oz; and a Leonard light salmon rod of 9 ft 6 in. and 7¼ oz.

The two Hardy rods have given me a quarter of a century of service. The Leonard is slightly less venerable, but I treasure it as an unsolicited gift for which I have never ceased to be grateful. It so happened that some years ago a non-angling friend, temporarily resident in New York as representative of the New Zealand Meat Board, gave to one of his American friends a copy of my earlier book on Taupo fishing. The American was Arthur Mills, proprietor of a celebrated tackle shop in downtown Manhattan.

Arthur Mills read the book and then told Joe Malcolm: 'Look, I'd like this guy Hintz to have one of my Leonard rods, and I hope he'll fish with it. I can rub some dust into the cork grip so that it will be classed as a used rod, free of Customs duty, if you can get it delivered to him.'

Joe wrote to inform me of the glad tidings and of the arrangements that he had made for the delivery of the rod. To this day, I do not suppose that he realises what a treasure he had accepted on my behalf. He probably knew that the Leonard rods were made by a subsidiary of Arthur Mills's firm, but I doubt whether he appreciated their comparative rarity, especially in New Zealand, and the mana that attaches to their name.

The rod arrived according to plan and with due reverence I took delivery of it from the captain of a Danish ship engaged in the Pacific trade. The captain, far from being a melancholy Dane, insisted on sealing the delivery transaction with our joint consumption of several bottles of chilled Tuborg lager.

The rod was a joy to handle, much lighter than either of my Hardy rods but unbelievably powerful and capable of handling a moderately heavy line. A few weeks after its delivery I took the handsome Leonard on its first expedition to the upper pools of the Waitahanui. The first real run of fish for the season had just entered the river.

I made the trip upstream by car with the precious rod firmly strapped to the left-hand door handles. I have never accustomed myself to rod clamp attachments on the roof of a car. I proceeded to a favourite pool known as Butler's Bend, entered the water and started to cast. The rod, so perfect in earlier practice, refused to function. It would not shoot even a yard of line. A swift inspection revealed the awful truth. One of the intermediate snake rings was partially dislodged from its silk tyings—obviously as the result of an encounter with some projecting scrub on the heavily overgrown car track.

There was I, some miles away from tying silk, wax and the other essentials for repair, and only the one rod with me. I rummaged through my pockets and mercifully found a small rubber band. I dismantled the rod and by some ingenious winding and looping managed to get the rubber band into position so that it held the dislodged rod ring fairly securely. Then, with gear re-assembled, I re-entered the water and on my very first cast hooked a fish.

I was in fear and trembling that the rod ring might again give way and that I might find myself in all sorts of trouble, I need not have worried. The rod took control of the fish and maintained control throughout a brisk battle. I was able to see for myself the swift responses of the undamaged tip section to every variation in pressure. I fought the final stages of the battle from the bank and the rod finally brought the fish virtually to my feet. As I eased the fish up on the sand, the fly fell out of its jaw. But there it was—a handsome Rainbow hen of 21 in. and 4½ lb. I walked back to my car and did not fish the Leonard again until the rod ring had been permanently and expertly repaired.

Only that one misadventure has befallen my treasured Leonard. It has landed for me fish up to 8½ lb in weight and today it remains as straight and true as it was when it left Arthur Mills's establishment in Park Place, off Lower Broadway. In the intervening years, on what used to be fairly frequent visits to or through New York, I invariably called on Arthur or his son Steve in Park Place and gave them news of the mounting tally standing to the credit of Arthur's handsome gift.

If I am proud of the Leonard and careful in its maintenance, I am equally proud of my two Hardy rods and bestow on them equal care and attention. All three rods have spare tips and on all of them the tips are changed over at monthly intervals. At one stage the Hardy 'Wood' suffered somewhat from my stupidity in fishing it for about three seasons with too heavy a line. It was during the years when terylene or dacron was beginning to replace silk in the manufacture of fly lines, and I did not appreciate at the time the difference that higher specific gravity would make in the pressure exerted on the rod during intensive sunk fly fishing. Both tips of the 'Wood' developed a distinct downward curve, but in neither of them did the cane show a sign of springing.

I took the rod with me to London on one of my regular visits, and the House of Hardy proved equal to the occasion. Split cane was still in reasonable supply and the rod was fitted with two brand new tips which, with a change to a less hawser-like line, are still as straight as a die.

I shudder to think what would happen today if any comparable degree of carelessness caused me to inflict damage on one or other of my three prized rods. The rod makers have moved so swiftly away from split cane to fibreglass that before long it will probably be impossible to replace a broken split cane tip at anything but prohibitive cost.

Yet I still cling to my split cane rods. I have fished occasionally with glass rods, both in New Zealand and in the United States, and I have been impressed with their lightness and their strength. But they seem to lack the living quality of split cane. There is something synthetic about them, both in appearance and in performance. Nevertheless, they seem destined to supplant split cane, just as split cane supplanted the earlier greenheart. The way in which the manufacturers have overcome the early tendency in fibre-glass rods to go soft and sloppy in action suggests that improvements in the new material will continue, so that before long the fisherman who appears on the water with a split-cane rod will be treated indulgently as a survival from a bygone era—or alternatively as an old square.

Until recently I used to think that the Vietnam war had speeded the change from split cane to fibreglass. All of us know that the best split cane—the only split cane from which quality rods were fashioned—came from Tonkin bamboo, and it was only natural to think that, as Tonkin was situated in North Vietnam, the prolonged hostilities had interrupted supplies and had given the fabricators of fibreglass their opportunity to capture the market.

The fact is that the bamboo commonly called 'Tonkin cane' comes from a small area in South China, not far from Canton. It is known to the growers as 'Ch'a Kon Chuk', or 'Tea-stick bamboo', and back before 1938 exports, chiefly through Hong Kong, were worth more than a million United States dollars a year. Whether Chairman Mao and his henchmen have discovered other uses for the tea-stick bamboo and are withholding it from bloated Western capitalist-imperialists, nobody seems to know. Possibly the small area of growth in the Kwangsi Province has become a collective farm and is producing something for the domestic market.

Whatever the reason, the Western capitalist-imperialists have undoubtedly succeeded in industrialising rod manu-facture, to the extent that, if I were starting off from scratch today, I should probably be fishing with a fibreglass rod. The weight-strength ratio of the new material has been perfected; particular rod models by any reputable manu-facturer can be standardised; action can be precisely and scientifically calculated; and spare sections can be held in stock for immediate replacement in the event of breakages.

Comparative costs also weigh heavily in favour of fibreglass.

On Taupo waters these days, the glass rod is much more in evidence than the split cane, so the visiting angler need have no fear about a critical scrutiny of 'mod' equipment. What really matters is not the rod, whether it be split cane or fibreglass, but the purpose for which it has been selected and the manner in which it is used.

The modern fashion is for rods that are not only light in weight but also much shorter than the instruments favoured by the Taupo veterans in the days of my novitiate when huge double-handers up to 16 ft in length were commonplace. The short-light fetish is not necessarily a bad thing so long as the rod is designed with sufficient strength to cope with the normal Taupo practice of fairly long casting and deep-sunk retrieving of the fly.

Lightweight reels with substantial line carrying capacity rank as essential. On my three prized rods I use Pflueger Medalist reels, 4 in. on the two Hardy rods and 3⅝ in. on the Leonard. There are other reels of comparable lightness and capacity, but I have remained faithful to the Pflueger Medalist because in nearly forty years of fishing I have never experienced any sort of reel trouble.

As with rods and all other fishing gear, reasonable maintenance counts for a lot. It pays to keep reels well oiled and greased and periodically to check all screw fittings and to tighten them as necessary. One common sight on Taupo waters always infuriates me. A fisherman will be wading knee-deep when he decides that something near the tip of his rod needs adjustment. He will promptly lower the butt under water while he performs the required task. He does not stop to think that his reel will inevitably collect highly abrasive pumice from the bottom, nor does he seem aware of the fact that, if his reel is properly oiled, a mixture of oil and water constitutes an extremely vicious cutting agent on most metal alloys.

One advantage of the modern, lightweight reel is that it is generally available with spare drums, a feature which the modern line manufacturer has not been slow to appreciate. Taupo fishing is predominantly sunk fly work, but variable water levels can often be encountered and at times it can prove disconcerting to be fishing with a line that sinks either too fast or too slow under the prevailing conditions. Again, fish may be discovered smelting, or surface-feeding on green beetle. In such circumstances, a sinking line is quite definitely a handicap.

Not so very long ago anglers the world over regarded British fly lines as supreme. That was in the days of oil-dressed silk lines and before the appearance of plastic-coated nylon, terylene and dacron. Now the American line manufacturers are probably, if anything, one jump ahead of the British. With the modern synthetics, they have developed lines that float ungreased and lines that, unweighted, sink like a stone. In between they have provided the slow sinking, the medium sinking and the sink-tip lines. On the debit side, they have also introduced the shooting head on monofilament—a combination that should be comprehensively banned on fly water.

The angler who puts his faith in a single multi-purpose outfit of rod and reel can still equip himself with fly lines for almost all conceivable conditions, particularly if he has the good sense to acquire spare drums for his one all-purpose reel. On three separate drums he can mount fast sinking, slow sinking and floating lines, and with the two spare drums disposed round his person he can be ready for any change in conditions that may call for a change in angling technique.

One point worth remembering is that the spare drums should be carried in suitable dust-proof and grit-proof bags. I may be pernickety to a fault, but nothing destroys my angling pleasures more than the rasping sound of a dirty reel.

It is a matter of personal choice whether the angler favours a weight-forward, double taper or level line. For Taupo fishing my preference is for the forward taper, once called torpedo head, and for my various reels I have an assortment of six lines by Scientific Anglers and Cortland, ranging from high density and extra fast sinking to sink-tip and floating. For dry fly work elsewhere I prefer a double taper Air-Cel line. Our style of sunk fly fishing at Taupo generally demands distance casting, and I am convinced that a good forward taper line of a weight suitable for the rod will add about five yards to the casting range of an angler of average proficiency.

The looping of lines also serves a most useful purpose. On the reel end of every fly line that I possess I have spliced a small loop of nylon backing. On the forward end of the backing or filler line I splice a larger loop, wide enough for the reel to pass through it. Thus I can engage or disengage line and backing at a moment's notice and change from one line to another with a minimum of delay.

Similarly I splice a small loop of backing to the forward end of the dressed fly line, so that line and cast can be simply looped together without complicated knotting.

Casts or leaders no longer present a problem. The early troubles with nylon monofilament have long since been overcome and the material is available from many manufacturers at consistently high quality. Many of us who recall the days of knotted silkworm gut must wonder at times how we managed to enjoy our fishing. Nylon of relatively fine gauge is infinitely stronger than natural gut of much heavier gauge. The material is so cheap that even such inevitable exasperations as wind knots give little real cause for worry. It saves time and trouble simply to discard a wind-knotted cast and to replace it with a fresh length of nylon from the convenient spool.

For my Taupo fishing, regardless of wind or water, I

never use nylon with a breaking strain heavier than 8 lb. Nor do I bother about tapered casts. A three-yard length of fine, level nylon provides a reasonably invisible link between the fly line and the fly, and experience teaches which of several recommended knots is best suited for attaching fly to leader. The double clinch knot seems to be as dependable as any.

Tapered casts or leaders can undoubtedly serve a useful purpose in dry fly fishing, but for sunk fly work they represent a superfluous refinement. Once I had occasion to curse such a leader with what I regarded at the time as a virtuoso performance in inspired profanity.

A very good American friend, Jimmy Flint, was fishing with me at Taupo after a spell on the Brown trout waters of Southland. He had only floating lines with him, so I detached from one of my rods a Pflueger reel with its customary sinking line and Jimmy was equipped for his Taupo fishing. When he returned the reel to me at the end of his visit, one of his own leaders was at the end of the line.

The reel went back on my Leonard rod, and on my next visit to the river it seemed a perfectly natural procedure to tie the fly of my choice on the end of Jimmy's leader. On the tackle thus assembled I promptly hooked a fish. It came out of the pool in three or four prodigious leaps, and I am still convinced, from the evidence of my own eyes, that it was the heaviest and most handsome fish that I have hooked since I became a permanent Taupo resident.

The fish charged out of the pool and round a bend. I forded the river at a known crossing and proceeded to play the fish in a long reach of clear water from the more or less unobstructed left bank. I played it, I suppose, for the best part of a quarter of an hour before the unrelenting pressure of the Leonard weakened it and gradually I reeled it in toward my own bank. There was a fringe of musk and watercress at the spot where I proposed to land it, and I applied a shade more rod pressure to bring the exhausted fish over the obstruction.

The cast pinged and the greater part of it came back to me. The fish, with my fly still in its jaw, righted itself and moved slowly out into the current. To this day I swear that it must have gone all of 10 lb. And then I looked closely at Jimmy's leader. It was one of those expensively tapered jobs, doubtless purchased in New York from the very donor of my rod. Had I realised that I was landing a heavy fish on a tapered leader, I would never have exerted that extra pressure.

After my spell of senseless cursing, I suddenly remembered old Harry Tahau and solemnly intoned his benediction: 'Good luck to the fish!'

Rods and reels, lines and leaders—all provide ample scope for individual preference and choice. My chief endeavour has been to indicate from personal experience the type of gear suitable for Taupo fishing. Flies fall into a different category and we shall deal with them later in some detail. But we can pause for a moment to consider not just the refinements of tackle but the manner in which selected tackle is employed.

Over the years I have been astonished to observe how many fishermen of considerable angling experience lack any real appreciation of the essential techniques of fly casting. They get out line and put a fly into the water some distance away, but with an expenditure of physical effort and with a strain on the rod that need never be accepted. A cricketer, a golfer or a tennis player, once he aspires to a reasonable degree of proficiency in his chosen sport, does not hesitate to submit himself to expert tuition and coaching. Far too many fly fishers try to advance by an individual process of trial and error and generally succeed in perpetuating error.

In various parts of the world skilled professionals teach fly-casting as an art. Yet the angling novice does not necessarily have to seek such expert tuition. Anglers basically are friendly folk and the beginner can learn much merely by watching a competent and experienced fly caster and then by asking for advice and instruction which in the vast majority of cases will be freely given. In addition, whole chapters of angling literature are devoted to the mechanics and dynamics of fly casting, copiously illustrated with photographs and diagrams. A study of these technical instructions can save hours and even years of frustrating effort and wasted energy.

I am no tournament caster, nor do I ever aspire to become one. But by study and practice over the years I have acquired the ability to lay out thirty yards of dressed line in front of me with reasonable precision and with a minimum of physical exertion. So I make bold to stress a few fundamentals of fly casting in the hope that they may prove useful not only to beginners but also to relative veterans who have become unconsciously the slaves of bad habits.

The first thing to appreciate in fly casting is that it is not the fly you cast, but the line. The weight and balance of the line provide the force to activate the fundamental spring that is built into the rod, so that the line itself can be shot forward, propelling the fly toward the desired objective.

The next thing to appreciate is that the rod, thus employed, must serve as an extension of the hand, wrist and forearm. With properly balanced gear and with an acceptance of this physical principle, muscular effort above the elbow should be reduced to a minimum.

Stance is also important. While the main muscular effort in casting should be exerted by forearm, wrist and hand, the upper arm from shoulder to elbow still plays its part and a certain degree of body rotation is inescapable. It goes without saying that an angler casting from a two-eyed stance, with both feet in line, cannot possibly achieve the muscular rhythm essential for easy and efficient operation of the equipment that he is using.

The right-handed caster should always stand with his left foot slightly advanced. Such a stance allows the upper part of the body to pivot easily, with the necessary balance for the forearm action.

For years I used to be horrified at the laboured efforts of an angling friend, now dead, to lay out a reasonable length of casting line. He was right-handed but, while casting, he would invariably stand with his right foot forward. To be able to cast respectably from such a stance he would have had to be double-jointed—which, as far as I know, he was not. He would thrash the water to foam, break innumerable rods and yet persist in physical effort that was clearly self-defeating.

One morning my friend and I had the Waitahanui Rip to ourselves and he was labouring away in his accustomed fashion. Finally I decided that I knew him well enough to offer him a word of advice.

'Peter,' I said, 'have you ever thought how difficult it is to cast with your right foot forward?'

'What do you mean?' said Peter.

'Well,' I explained, 'standing like that you practically lock the whole of the right side of your body. You can't possibly get the proper swing or rhythm. Try standing with your left foot forward.'

Peter altered his stance, completed his retrieve and cast again. With four throws he laid out his full fishing length of line, whereas earlier it had taken him seven.

'By Jove,' he said, 'that does make a difference.'

For a quarter of an hour or so he continued to cast tolerably well, and then his right foot started to inch forward. Before long he was back in his old, clumsy, impossible stance, and his line was flopping miserably on the water. Old and bad habits certainly die hard.

Charles Ritz and other eminent authors have written about the refinements of fly casting in great detail. A study of their illustrated writings can profit even an experienced and reasonably proficient fisherman, for it is the habit of experts to transform an acquired art into an exact science.

My purpose is to simplify. First of all, a comfortable and balanced stance, with the body slightly inclined so that the foot opposite the casting arm is placed forward. Secondly, a proper grip on the rod, with the thumb on the top of the cork grip and pointing toward the tip of the rod. A steady, upward movement for the back cast, with the rod deliberately checked at the perpendicular and with the left hand, holding the line between reel and butt ring, purposefully lowered to its full extent. Then the forward cast, with the rod checked just above the horizontal and with the left hand still exerting downward pressure until retrieved line is shot from the hand.

One of the most common faults in casting is to raise the line-holding hand simultaneously with the rod-holding hand. Unless the line-holding hand maintains a continuous downward pressure, part of the rod action is wasted in straightening loose line between the rod rings and there is a loss of energy in the transmission of the weight of the line to the spring of the rod.

Many of the acknowledged experts have perfected the art of the double haul, pulling downward on the line first on the back cast and then again on the forward cast. They achieve remarkable results. I do not consciously practise the double haul, but I probably approach the same end by making sure that while I am casting my left hand maintains a continuous downward pressure on my line. Rhythm and timing come with practice and must always be adjusted to the strength and direction of the wind. Like most anglers, I would sooner cast into a moderate head wind than have a strong wind at my back. In my experience, the worst wind of all for a right-handed caster is the wind that comes from over your right shoulder.

Now a word or two for the beginner. Never try to lift

off the water for the back cast an excessive length of sunk line. To do so is to invite, sooner or later, a sprung tip and expensive rod repairs. Taupo trout take often on the swing of the fly across a current, but more often on the retrieve, and it pays to retrieve line, either by coiling or gathering in the left hand, until only about three yards or so of line, plus cast and fly, extend beyond the rod tip. The next step, barring a strike from a fish, is to practise a roll cast that will bring the short length of line, cast and fly onto the surface of the water preparatory for the back cast.

The art of shooting line from the left hand on the forward cast comes only with practice. No hard and fast rules can be laid down to determine the precise moment at which retrieved line should be released to go whistling through the rod rings. It is something sensed through the action of rod and line, but once the art is acquired the angler with well-balanced gear should be able to lay out his maximum casting length of line in two, or at the most, three casts.

Some fishermen coil line on the retrieve; others gather it in the palm of the left hand. I cling to the belief, probably mistaken, that a gathered retrieve imparts a more lifelike action to the fly under water, but some of the most competent and successful anglers of my acquaintance habitually coil on the retrieve, so it would be foolish to wax dogmatic on the point.

A fish that takes on the swing of the fly more often than not hooks itself. On the retrieve it is a different matter. The best course of action is to strike swiftly and firmly with the left hand, rather than with the rod tip, and then to throw however much line has been retrieved into the water. If the fish runs, it will swiftly drag all the loose line through the rod rings with much less risk of a snarl than if the line were fed out from the hand. If the fish seems reluctant to run, it may be necessary for the fisherman to move backward, paying out loose line by hand through the butt ring and trying to keep the line as tight as possible until the fish is on the reel. As soon as it feels the reel, the fish will generally make up its mind to take some violent form of action.

In playing a hooked fish I normally try to get my feet on dry land as soon as I possibly can. Once on bank or beach, the fisherman has some freedom for manoeuvre and with a stubborn fish can often succeed in walking it out, moving slowly backward where the terrain permits and then walking briskly forward and reeling in to shorten line.

Over recent years I have noticed a growing tendency among Taupo anglers to play their fish from bank or beach with the rod held horizontally across the body. I suppose the theory is that the reduced angle of pull lessens the risk of dragging the hook from its hold in the mouth of the fish. It always seems to me to be a rather awkward business. I prefer to play my fish with the rod held as nearly as possible in the perpendicular. The upward pull certainly helps to subdue a fish that happens to have been hooked in the upper jaw.

None of us, unfortunately, can contrive always to hook fish in that part of the mouth where the hook itself will take firmest hold. Probably everything depends on the angle at which the fish approaches the fly. I have often been tempted to think that what we describe as a pull or a tug, or 'taking short', is caused by the fish charging at the fly in the opposite direction from the retrieve, so that it fouls the cast before it hits the fly and swiftly turns away to leave a dejected angler bemoaning a missed strike. Again, a fish may approach the fly from astern, grab at the tail, take short and escape the point and barb of the hook. Quite conceivably, most fish that get themselves firmly hooked approach the fly from the side. But there is nothing that the angler can do about it.

One thing is certain: If a fish happens to get itself hooked through what passes for its tongue, it will perform most violently. As far as I know, the marine biologists have never listed the tongue of the trout as one of its main sensory organs, but in my experience any fish hooked in the tongue fights harder, longer and more fiercely than one that has been hooked in the jaw.

Quite recently I hooked a good fish in what I regarded as a most unusual fashion. It took the fly in one of my favourite pools on the Waitahanui and fought strongly, with several spectacular leaps clean out of the water. But for some reason I felt that I had the fish firmly under control. Eventually I landed it and, after killing it, I had to perform a major post-mortem operation. The fish had been hooked in the roof of the mouth and the point of the hook had emerged through its left nostril. It was a fresh-run hen fish of 7 lb, 23½ in. long and with a condition factor of 58, but from the way the hook was lodged its fate must have been sealed from the outset.

I suppose I had always taken it for granted that the two small apertures on a trout's head served as nostrils, but the hooking of a fish in this unusual fashion sent me searching among my various works of reference for some precise anatomical knowledge. I learned that the trout's pair of nostrils lead into nasal sacs which have no connection with the mouth; that very little is known about the function of the nostrils in relation to a sense of smell; and that 'the part of the trout's brain dealing with the sense of smell is relatively small and poorly developed.'

None of this information seemed to count for very much against the established fact that I had somehow managed to hook and land a trout by the nose.

In the matter of flies, the Taupo fisherman can choose from a brave collection of locally devised patterns, with a few imported specimens added for good measure. Strictly speaking, the flies are lures, designed to simulate under water the movement of the small fish on which the trout feed. Exact imitation does not matter. The sunk fly attracts

178

by shape, size and movement—and the greatest of these is movement.

The early Taupo Rainbows and Browns were hooked almost exclusively on standard Scottish salmon flies, if not on spinners, but gradually over the years local patterns evolved, based to some extent on American streamer flies, but with variations in construction that made them rather more effective. The 'tail-and-hackle' type, the 'Killer' type and the 'fixed wing streamer' all appear to be largely local inventions.

Taupo flies are tied over a wide range of hook sizes, varying from No. 2 or even No. 1/0 for night fishing to Nos. 4, 6 and 8 for daylight hours. Some patterns can be best tied on extra long shank hooks, but the standard type of hook, with either down-turned or up-turned eye, generally suffices, even for such an exotic specimen as the American Muddler Minnow.

Sooner or later, most trout fishermen aspire to tie their own flies and, with all due respect to the tackle dealers, often succeed in producing better specimens than the mass-produced shop variety. The choice of fly for particular conditions is always a matter of individual preference, and the flies that a fisherman ties for himself naturally reflect the faith that he reposes in certain established patterns.

For what it is worth, I propose to list the dozen patterns that I use most frequently on Taupo waters and to prescribe their dressings. They may not be every Taupo fisherman's choice, but, tied carefully and fished competently, they will ensure for the newcomer to our waters his fair quota of fish.

The flies are Hamill's Killer, Lord's Killer, Parsons' Glory, Split Partridge, Muddler Minnow, Rabbit (three varieties), Tail and Hackle (so described because in different parts of the Taupo district the fly is known as a Hairy Dog, a Fuzzy Wuzzy or a Mrs Simpson), Red Setter, Mallard and Grizzly Green. Old favourites like the Leslie's Lure, the

Orbit, the Tiger Ross and the Tamiti seem to have gone out of fashion these days, but then fashions in trout flies, as in most other things, are constantly changing. I have given only one possible smelt fly, the Grizzly Green, but others can be easily copied.

Here are my recommended dressings:

HAMILL'S KILLER

Hook sizes 2, 4 and 6.

Tag Silver tinsel thread.

Tail Black squirrel tail, projecting about $\frac{3}{4}$ in. from tag and with a strip of golden pheasant tippet tied in at the butt on either side. The tail should be firmly anchored along the shank of the hook.

Body Red or yellow wool.

Wings Paired tips of dyed green partridge hackles, tied in on either side of the body with both tying silk and body material. From three to five pairs of feathers will be needed, depending on the size of the hook.

Hackle None.

Head Black.

Remarks A splendid all-purpose fly for any conditions of light or water. Red body preferred.

LORD'S KILLER

Hook sizes 2, 4 and 6.

Tag Silver tinsel thread.

Whisks Strands of dyed red cock hackle or red silk.

Tail Black squirrel, tied as for Hamill's Killer but without golden pheasant tippets.

Body Red, yellow, orange or green wool.

Wings Paired small feathers from woodcock wings, tied in on either side of the body with both tying silk and body material. The pairs of feathers will vary in number according to the size of the hook.

Hackle None.

Head Black.

Remarks The Lord's Killer on a No. 2 hook with a red body makes a splendid night fly. Other colours on smaller hooks for day fishing.

PARSONS' GLORY

Hook sizes 4, 6 and 8.

Tag Gold tinsel thread.

Whisks Dyed red hackle fibres.

Ribbing Gold tinsel twist.

Body Yellow mohair or wool.

Wing-tail Honey grizzle neck hackles, paired back to back, with fibres from lower section of quill stripped for the length of the body and with the unstripped tips of the hackles projecting about $\frac{1}{2}$ in. to $\frac{3}{4}$ in. from butt of body. Hackle stalks tied in at the head of the body and ribbing passed between upright hackle fibres to anchor wing section to body.

Hackle Honey grizzle.

Cheeks Jungle cock.

Topping Golden pheasant crest over all.

Head Black.

Remarks Still the best of the old-time Taupo lures. Particularly effective on falling water.

SPLIT PARTRIDGE

Hook sizes 4 and 6.

Tag Silver or gold tinsel thread.

Ribbing Silver or gold tinsel twist.

Body Green, yellow or orange wool.

Wing Partridge tail split down centre of quill and with tip of tail discarded; split wing sections assembled back to back, with forward end of quill projecting slightly beyond butt of body; bare quill sections tied in at head and ribbing passed between upright fibres to anchor wing to body. Ribbing and tag silver for green body, gold for yellow and orange.

Hackle Light furnace.

Head Black.

Remarks A most dependable fly. Tied fine, serves well for smelting fish.

MUDDLER MINNOW

Hook sizes 4 and 6; and 6 XLS.

Tail Brown mottled turkey tied in like a short wing just before the bend of the hook.

Body Flat gold tinsel tied in first about two-thirds of the way to the eye of the hook, wound down to the tail and evenly back to the starting point and firmly secured.

Streamer Small bunch of reddish brown calf hair, with a smaller bunch of white calf hair on top, tied in at head of body.

Wing Brown mottled turkey tied in at head of body as for standard wet fly.

Hackle Small bunch of fine deer hair tied in below wing and under shank of hook, with ends reaching as far as hook point.

Head Successive bunches of deer body hair spun with the tying silk round naked shank of hook from wing to eye. Five or six bunches of hair may have to be applied. The deer hair is then close clipped to form a ruff head of short fibres right to the eye of the hook.

Remarks A tried and tested North American pattern which works well under Taupo conditions.

RABBIT

Hook sizes 4 and 6.

Tag Tinsel thread, silver for green body, gold for yellow or orange.

Ribbing Tinsel twist, as for tag.

Body Chenille, green, yellow or orange.

Wing A strip of rabbit pelt about 1 in. long and ⅛ in. wide, with the fur in good condition; fur removed from skin for about ⅛ in. at head and bare skin firmly lodged with tying silk at head of body; pelt then firmly bound on top of body by ribbing through fur fibres.

Hackle Optional, but seldom used.

Head Red for green body, black for yellow and orange.

Remarks A simple but effective fly under most conditions, with the Orange Rabbit often deadly against running trout in winter.

CLARET

Hook size 4.

Tag Gold tinsel thread.

Whisks Golden pheasant tippet.

Ribbing Gold tinsel twist.

Body Claret chenille.

Wing Strip of dark dyed rabbit pelt, tied as in standard Rabbit fly.

Hackle Dyed claret cock.

Head Black.

Remarks An excellent fly for sunset and dusk.

BLACK AND ORANGE

Hook size 4.

Tag Gold tinsel thread.

Whisks Golden pheasant tippet.

Ribbing Gold tinsel twist.

Body Equal sections of orange and black chenille, with the black section at the head.

Wing As for Claret.

Hackle Coch-y-Bondhu.

Head Black.

Remarks Recommended for dawn fishing.

TAIL AND HACKLE

Hook sizes 2 and 4.

Tag Tinsel thread, silver for red and green bodies, gold for yellow and orange.

Whisks Two short strands of red silk.

Tail Black squirrel, projecting about ¾ in. from butt and anchored well along shank of hook.

Body hackles Two black cock hackles.

Body Red, green, yellow or orange wool, tied in three equal sections, with a body hackle wound on at the head of tail and middle sections.

Throat hackle Black, rather longer in fibre than body hackles.

Head Black.

Remarks The red-bodied fly, tied on a No. 2 hook, is a most effective night fly. The other colours are useful on dull days and in discoloured water.

RED SETTER

Hook sizes 4 and 6.

Tag Gold tinsel thread.

Tail Reddish brown squirrel tied in as for Tail and Hackle type.

Body hackle Rhode Island red.

Body Orange wool in two sections, with the body hackle wound on between them.

Throat hackle Rhode Island red, rather longer in fibre than body hackle.

Head Black.

Remarks A useful fly for late autumn and winter fishing when the trout are running to spawn. It is normally fished deep and fairly slow.

Hook sizes 4 and 6.

Tag Silver or gold tinsel thread.

Tail Black squirrel as for Killer type.

Body Yellow, green or orange wool in two sections.

Wings Two pairs of grey breast feathers from a mallard drake; one pair tied in on either side of the hook at the head of the butt section of body, the other pair similarly at the head.

Head Black.

Remarks A favourite fly on the big pools of the Tongariro River. Tied fine and with a body of flat silver tinsel, it is often effective as a smelt fly.

GRIZZLY GREEN

Hook sizes 4, 6 and 8.

Tag Silver tinsel thread.

Whisks Dyed red cock hackle fibres.

Tail A pair of barred grizzle hackle tips, about $\frac{3}{4}$ in. long and tied in by the quills along the top of the shank so that the hackle fibres are in a vertical plane.

Body Light green wool in two sections.

Body hackle Barred grizzle wound on between the two body sections.

Throat hackle Barred grizzle, rather more generous in size than body hackle.

Head Red.

Remarks My wife would never forgive me if I omitted this fly from my favoured list. It is her standby when the fish are in the river. The fly is really a variation of a standard pattern known as the Dorothy, which is similar to the Parsons' Glory but tied with barred grizzle hackle feathers in place of honey grizzle and lacking the jungle cock and golden pheasant.

I do not pretend for a moment that my selected list of fly dressings will meet all the needs or all the fancies of the average Taupo fisherman. If he ties his own flies he will almost certainly introduce his own variations, both in materials and in methods of construction. Yet the beginner always has to make a start somewhere, and he can gain from the experience of others.

All of us who fish for trout accumulate more flies than we can ever hope to use. Occasionally we are tempted to collect gadgets as well, although rarely to the extent that seems to be common among American fishermen.

I am not greatly given to gadgetry, but there are some items of American angling equipment that command respect. First and foremost I would place the typical American fishing vest, a sleeveless garment of waist length and consisting almost entirely of pockets. I bought one in New York some years ago, wore it almost to shreds and now use a second vest of a different make and even superior design.

It supplies me with about fifteen pockets of varying sizes, so that I am never on the water without at least three well-filled fly boxes on my person, plus a couple of spools of nylon, spring balance and coiled metal measuring tape, windproof cigarette lighter and cigarette case. Extra pockets are spacious enough to carry a couple of spare reel-drums or even a spare reel, and the entire back of the vest is built as a pocket that will comfortably hold a lightweight waterproof jacket or sweater. The whole garment is really a fishing bag converted into an article of clothing. I would be lost without it.

Another item of equipment that I favour is an American angler's clip, an instrument rather like an outsize nail clipper and much more useful than a pair of scissors for trimming surplus nylon ends after a fly has been attached to a leader. The clip also incorporates a hook disgorger, a small screwdriver, a stiletto and that indispensable aid to a thirsty fisherman—a bottle opener. The gadget can be hung round the neck on a piece of cord and is always available for action.

The one other piece of equipment which I regard as essential is a weighted wooden priest that slips into the front pocket of my body waders. It always seems to me to be preferable to a stick or a stone for administering the last rites to such a worthy adversary as a vanquished trout.

A sport as individual and as personal as fly fishing challenges the fly fisher to take a pride in the gear that he assembles for his chosen pastime. Much of it, if he cares for it properly, will outlive him. Some debate has been proceeding recently in respected angling publications regarding the ultimate ownership of a favourite rod with which the late G. E. M. Skues practised the art of which he was an acknowledged master.

Both the angling clubs of which I am a distant member make a practice of holding annual rummage sales, and often rods, reels and flies that could be classed as collectors' pieces are put up for auction. Mercifully, I do not know the final fate of my own treasured tackle—whether it will be sent to London or New York for sale or whether it will be disposed of among friends and relatives. Some of it may possess historical value, not because of original ownership but rather because of irreplaceable quality.

All I hope is that, after I have cast my final fly, my rods and tackle will be acquired by someone who will use them, someone who will care for them and someone who will gain from them as much joy as they have given me over all my angling years.

IX

CAUDAL FIN

'A Wet Posterior and an Empty Creel!'

Fisherman's Luck dogs all of us from time to time, and of recent months I seem to have been getting more than my fair share of it. I have been working on the final draft of this book for the duration of a long, dry, Taupo summer during which the reduced flow from the tributary rivers and streams has resulted in the most disastrous shoaling at the river mouths. To make matters worse, the blackmailing Arabs, through their imposed energy crisis, have forced our own electricity people to lower artificially still further the level of a lake already lowered by natural causes. Their aim has been to release enough water from Nature's reservoir to feed and keep in operation the string of hydro-electric power stations down the Waikato River and thus to conserve precious oil.

One school of thought, studying cause and effect, seeks to trace the origins of the whole sorry business back to Biblical times. The pundits of this particular school argue, with tongue in cheek, that if only Moses, having led the children of Israel out of captivity in Egypt and across the Red Sea, had turned right instead of left, the Israelis, not the Arabs, would have had all that lovely oil and our present troubles would never have arisen.

Regardless of cause, the effect of a falling lake level and shoaling river mouths has been a season of the most patchy fly fishing within living memory. Trout will not normally congregate in shoaled and silted water, and the Taupo Rainbows during the past summer have remained true to form, staying out in deep water well beyond the range of all but boat fishermen and probably often frequenting those intermediate zones in which boat fishing is prohibited, but which are still well beyond the casting range of wading fly fishermen.

Yet the trout must still run into the rivers to spawn. Doubtless they have been cruising about and feeding as best they can, waiting for autumn rains to bring freshes to the rivers before the vanguard of spawners charges across the inhospitable shoals of silt into the relative comfort of clean, running water.

It so happens that just as the unpredictable autumn runs could have been expected to begin I was suddenly removed, at least temporarily, from the angling scene. Out of the blue, I was stricken with peritonitis, requiring emergency and drastic surgery, and the long, slow haul of convalescence still stretches ahead of me. I simply go through the necessary physical exertions and await the day, not too far distant I hope, when I can next take a rod to the river.

Meanwhile I can reflect at leisure on the whys and

wherefores of fishless days. In the present circumstances, it would be both foolish and incurably selfish to argue that a desperate need for electric power should be subordinated to the uncompromising requirements of anglers. An energy crisis demands emergency measures. Nevertheless it is still possible to look to the future and to demonstrate how unwise it is to subject out natural water resources to intolerable strains.

It is at such a point that your angler who has graduated as a conservationist must make his voice heard. He must join with those who insist that alternative sources of energy should be found to reduce demands on Nature that Nature at times may not be willing to heed. In any river system too great a reliance on hydro-electric development, or on irrigation projects for that matter, can produce harmful effects right back to the source. Where that source happens to be the natural reservoir of a great lake, artificial variations and fluctuations in levels and draw-off can produce unpredictable effects. Clean water can be rendered foul; noxious weed growth can be promoted and eutrophication speeded; a lovely lake can degenerate into a swamp.

In many parts of the world we have seen how fishermen have joined together to protect their fishing not just in their own interests, not just in the interests of future generations of fishermen, but in a wider sense to preserve for their fellow men the benison of clean water and an open countryside.

Within comparatively recent years, the angling conservationists of the British Isles and of North America have made a tremendous impact on community life by insisting that human ignorance and squalor, industrial recklessness and commercial avarice should no longer be permitted to foul a precious legacy that has existed since the dawn of time. The impact has been strong and benignant enough already to rescue some rivers and lakes from virtual extinction and to halt, if not remove, the threat to others.

Angling conservationists act, in the main, to preserve and protect their chosen sport, to ensure that trout and salmon still run in the rivers, to insist that the many dependent life cycles in the whole natural process are safeguarded and sustained. In doing so, they know that the trout itself is a fastidious creature, intolerant of foul and polluted water, and that mankind, in a society that is not only affluent but also effluent, must be equally fastidious for its own survival.

In a country as remote and as sparsely populated as New Zealand the threat to our lakes and rivers may not yet be as serious as it has become in older and more crowded lands. Nevertheless in certain areas the incipient threat has arisen. Trout fishermen, by seeking to maintain the quality of their sport in all available waters, can help to keep those waters clean and undefiled.

As matters stand, I shall not worry unduly about fishless days if only I can rest assured that the call for clean water has not fallen on deaf ears. Fish or no fish, lakes and rivers and streams are too precious an adornment of the landscape, too basic an essential for life itself, to be wantonly sacrificed.

Only a few days ago, not long after I had emerged from hospital, friends from Auckland came to stay with us. As a Waitahanui veteran, Hutch spent most of his time on the river. In my enfeebled state I could not join him, but on his return from the river one evening he recounted an experience that delighted me.

Walking from one pool to another, Hutch had encountered a stranger, similarly fishless. They passed the time of day and mutually bemoaned the apparent absence of fish from the river. The stranger told Hutch that he came from Tasmania and that this was the fourth successive year that he had visited New Zealand to fish the Waitahanui.

'Well,' said Hutch, 'it's tough this year, all right, but you must have had plenty of fish in the past three years.'

'Not at all,' replied the Tasmanian. 'Four visits in four

years, and I haven't yet landed and killed a Taupo trout. But I love this river, and I just love to fish.'

There speaks a true fisherman.

Some folk may be mystified by the title that I have given to this brief epilogue. They may not know that 'caudal fin' is the term used by marine biologists to describe the tail end of a fish. In its present context as a chapter heading, 'Caudal Fin' signifies, quite simply, the end of my tale.